He Has Shown You What is Good

He Has Shown You What is Good

Old Testament Justice Then and Now

The Trinity Lectures, Singapore, 2011

H.G.M. Williamson

WIPF & STOCK · Eugene, Oregon

HE HAS SHOWN YOU WHAT IS GOOD
Old Testament Justice Here and Now

Copyright © 2012 H.G.M. Williamson. All rights reserved. Except for brief quotations in critical publications or reviews, no part of this book may be reproduced in any manner without prior written permission from the publisher. Write: Permissions, Wipf and Stock Publishers, 199 W. 8th Ave., Eugene, OR 97401.

Published by permission of The Lutterworth Press, P.O. Box 60, Cambridge, CB1 2NT, United Kingdom

Wipf & Stock
An imprint of Wipf and Stock Publishers
199 W. 8th Avenue, Suite 3
Eugene OR, 97401
www.wipfandstock.com

ISBN 13: 978-1-62032-686-2

Manufactured in the U.S.A.

Contents

Preface   7
1. The Task in Hand   9
2. Divine Justice and Natural Justice   22
3. The Individual and Social Justice   44
4. Prophetic Justice   64
5. Messianic Justice   90
6. He Has Shown You What is Good   104

Bibliography   110
Index of Biblical References   111
General Index   114

Preface

It was a great honour to be invited to deliver the inaugural series of Trinity Lectures, a biennial series sponsored by Trinity Theological College, Singapore, which addresses a major current issue from a dogmatic or biblical perspective. These lectures are part of the College's ministry to the wider church community in Singapore in response to their generous support of several senior positions in the College. It has therefore been my aim throughout to speak and to write in ways that will be widely accessible to those who may not themselves be specialists in biblical studies but who share the belief that, when properly interpreted, the Bible is still of relevance to the framing of Christian beliefs and lifestyle. (Occasionally, more technical questions are addressed in the footnotes, but these can easily be ignored by those to whom they are of no interest.) As I shall try to make clear, this raises even more problems in relation to the Old Testament than the New, but that does not mean that the challenge should be shirked.

My wife and I were very generously hosted during our week-long stay in Singapore in July 2011, and I wish to put on record my gratitude to the College Principal, The Rev. Dr Ngoel Foong Nghlan, The Dean of Studies, Professor Tan Kim Huat, and my former student and long-term friend, Professor Gordon Wong. With all their colleagues they made us extremely welcome and it was, of course, stimulating to discuss occasionally differing perceptions of the subject of the lectures owing to the different social circumstances of England and Singapore. If the thesis that I put forward here is anywhere near the mark, however, that diversity is precisely something that should be welcomed and embraced as leading to a more contextually-based application of some fundamental biblical principles.

After I had accepted the invitation to lecture and had agreed upon the topic, I was providentially invited to lecture at the 2010 Vacation Term for Biblical Study in Oxford. This gave me a useful opportunity to sketch out the lectures and to receive valuable feedback at a stage of preparation that still allowed ample time for revision and improvement. My thanks are therefore due to the organizers and the participants in that year's programme.

I am happy to record that the preparation of this material gave me some surprises and led me to modify some previously unexamined presuppositions. My hope is that those who read this book may be similarly stimulated to think through afresh what the Old Testament may have to say to a topic which is often more frequently discussed than enacted.

1
The Task in Hand

The call for justice has become pervasive in the twenty-first century world. Indeed, it has reached the point where the word seems to be emptied of any real meaning. It is invoked by people on all sides of every argument to justify their position, regardless of the merits of their case or the means that they use to arrive at their goals. It has virtually become a legitimizing cover for 'getting what I want'.

In the present book I am particularly interested in the use of the term in the church. It is understandably a topic which has raised a good deal of interest over the years, not least by those who want to emphasize the degree to which the Bible has a distinctive contribution to make to the development of policy as well as to the formation of individual or personal lifestyles. The considerable success of the 'Jubilee 2000' campaign is a good example of this, though of course that is only one among many. Concerns for fair trade, smaller debt relief charities, human rights organizations and a myriad other valuable causes routinely appeal to one or another scriptural saying or principle. Sometimes, indeed, these seem to have become such an ingrained part of our cultural heritage that many who use them have probably forgotten — if ever they were aware — where they first originated.

Without in any way wanting to denigrate or belittle the valuable work that is promoted under the banner of justice, I sometimes observe the possibility that there can develop a danger of self-satisfaction in claiming to have fulfilled some higher, because biblical, injunction. The use of slogans bedevils church life as much as political life and it can be harmful. A text or two taken out of context is used to brand one course of action, and before we know what is happening there is a temptation to criticize those who may see things somewhat differently. Such a narrow and restricted understanding of the riches that are to be found within the diversity of scripture makes popularizing politicians of us all, with the woeful divisions into groups that almost become sects in consequence.

In order to counter this danger, there is a need, therefore, to reflect on the ways in which scripture can be more fruitfully engaged. The Old Testament, with which I am here primarily concerned, is a work not just of many different types of literature but one which may have been written over a period approaching a thousand years. During those centuries the many writers lived in politically and culturally variegated circumstances, whether in a sovereign independent state, or in a vassal and tribute-paying state, or in forced or voluntary exile or diaspora, or as a minor province in a world empire that effectively meant that they were a colony. Allocating the various books and parts of books of the Old Testament to one or another of these situations is not always easy, but it stands to reason that the impact on the topic of justice must have been considerable.

To put the matter at its simplest, the opportunities for implementing justice on a national level will have varied widely according to the degree of political independence that the nation enjoyed, while at the level of the individual the social and economic circumstances in Judah, Babylon or elsewhere were clearly so different from one another that the scope for manoeuvre must have been significantly impacted. In addition, it is probable that circumstances will have developed over the course of time, so that

1. The Task in Hand

the expectations for the implementation of justice will also have changed. To overlook such obvious matters in the interests of a superficially unified blueprint for action turns out, paradoxically, to be impoverishing. Flattening the rich variety of scripture — a variety that addresses many different possible scenarios and situations — has a tendency to reduce the imaginative application of the vision for justice to a checklist of platitudes which we can tick off as though we had achieved all that is required. As we shall see, however, an appreciation of the dynamism of the scripture's portrayal in fact heightens the challenge, as well as the encouragement, to more creative thinking on this crucial topic.

This widespread confusion should not deter us, however, from trying to arrive at a more legitimate understanding and implementation. I am aware that debates about justice are conducted at the highest intellectual level in works that challenge most of the rest of us as readers.[1] In the present book, however, I am concerned to engage with the topic at a far more accessible level. On the one hand, for reasons that I shall explain in a moment, I want to narrow the focus of discussion to what we should generally call social justice. Not only is this a prominent feature of the Old Testament writings; it also has the advantage of being sufficiently explicit to enable me to investigate the particular question that I have in mind in a manageable way.

---

1 I need only refer for illustration to the great works, often hailed as classics, of John Rawls, *A Theory of Justice* (Cambridge, MA: Harvard University Press, 1971), and *Justice as Fairness: A Restatement*, ed. Erin Kelly (Cambridge, MA: Harvard University Press, 2001), and of Amartya Sen, *The Idea of Justice* (London: Allen Lane, 2009). From the more specifically Christian perspective, see the rather different approach of Oliver O'Donovan, *The Ways of Judgment* (Grand Rapids, Michigan: Eerdmans, 2005). He recognizes the variety of senses of justice, but adopts a more rigorous line than will be favoured here. For more accessible introductions to the varieties of justice, see Michael J. Sandel, *Justice: What's the Right Thing to Do?* (London: Allen Lane, 2009), and Walter J. Houston, *Justice— The Biblical Challenge* (London: Equinox, 2010), 2–4.

On the other hand, rather than just seeking to arrive at a definition of social justice, which might then be set alongside others for comparison and contrast, my aim is to ask the more fundamental question: how, according to the biblical writers, do we know what is the socially just thing to do in any given set of circumstances? This is an important question but one which people rarely consider. It is all very well preaching sermons or writing books about the practice of justice in the biblical world. The danger is that we stop there and conclude that we have met the conditions. The nature of society and the way of life in ancient Israel were so very different from that in the modern world that a narrow biblical description can stop short of asking the more pressing questions of how to apply those insights to the modern world of capitalist enterprise, of global travel and trade, of warfare and violence on a scale which even the ancient Assyrians could not have imagined, of democratic institutions at national and local levels, and of media by television, radio, print and internet communication which now dominate and often, it seems, manipulate public opinion.

None of this is even remotely envisaged by the Bible and yet it makes much of the world in which we live into what it is. How, then, can we use biblical modes of thinking to inform our modern choices? Is it arbitrary or are there some principles that will help us? My exploration of some significant passages in the Old Testament with these questions in mind will, I hope, suggest the beginnings of an answer. Of course, from a Christian point of view this would need to be supplemented, and perhaps modified, by perspectives based on the New Testament. But if I am right in the line of argument that I shall advance, we shall see that this in fact takes its perfectly natural place in the biblical picture as a whole.

Narrowing the field

It is well known among biblical scholars that there is a pair of Hebrew words that are frequently combined to suggest more or less what we mean by social justice. In English translations

1. The Task in Hand

they are usually rendered 'justice and righteousness'. In Hebrew the two words are *mishpat* and *tsedaqah*.[2] Each of these words on its own is of rich and wide-ranging meaning which we cannot trace further here. While 'justice' and 'righteousness' are their commonest English equivalents, a glance at any reputable Bible dictionary will quickly reveal that even these grand words are approximate at best and in many ways overly restrictive.[3] Even so, while the combination is most indicative for our topic (and of course this includes examples where the two words are used each in parallel lines in poetry), we shall find that their occurrence individually (including related forms from the same roots), as well as with one or two other key terms, can be taken from the context (e.g. when dealing with relationships between people) to be also a useful guide.

These two words have often been commented on as central to our topic by scholars who in other respects differ widely from one another. Probably the fullest scholarly treatment (though by no means the only one) is that of Moshe Weinfeld, and I shall refer to his work from time to time in what follows to provide more detailed support of points that I necessarily touch on more briefly.[4] However, we might note

---

2 For convenience sake, I use here and throughout this book a simple form of transliteration that may be easily followed by those who do not know Hebrew even though I am well aware that from a technically formal point of view it is not strictly accurate. In the present instance, we are concerned, of course, with the hendiadys משפט וצדקה a phrase which additionally in poetry can be distributed over parallel lines.

3 See, for instance, B. Johnson, 'מִשְׁפָּט', in G. Johannes Botterweck, Helmer Ringgren and Heinz-Josef Fabry (eds.), *Theological Dictionary of the Old Testament* (Grand Rapids: Eerdmans, 1998), ix. 86–98, and David J. Reimer, 'צדק', in Willem A. VanGemeren (ed.), *The New International Dictionary of Old Testament Theology and Exegesis* (Carlisle: Paternoster, 1997), iii. 744–69.

4 Moshe Weinfeld, *Social Justice in Ancient Israel and in the Ancient Near East* (Jerusalem: Magnes, 1995). Note should be taken also of the substantial response to some aspects of Weinfeld's work (though not, I think, in ways that are unhelpful to my general argument) by Bernard

that it is also attended to carefully in less technical works,[5] and I discovered recently that it is also used fully in Miranda's influential and radical work of a previous generation.[6] In the course of his discussion (on page 93, with full references on p. 107) Miranda summarizes that the two words appear as a direct pair in thirty-one passages while they appear a further twenty-three times in strict synonymous parallelism in poetry.

The reason for thinking that these words are almost a technical term for social justice comes from those passages where their content is more fully spelt out.[7] In Job 29, for instance, Job lists what were clearly considered to be the standard and well-recognized acts of one who was acting in a wholly just manner, and in the course of the passage he states that they are in accordance with *justice* and *righteousness* (italicized here for clarity's sake):

> ... because I delivered the poor who cried,
> and the orphan who had no helper.

Jackson, 'Justice and Righteousness in the Bible: Rule of Law or Royal Paternalism?', *Zeitschrift für altorientalische und biblische Rechtsgeschichte* 4 (1998), 218–62, and '"Law" and "Justice" in the Bible', *Journal of Jewish Studies* 49 (1998), 218–29.

5 See, for instance, Christopher J.H. Wright, *Living as the People of God: The Relevance of Old Testament Ethics* (Leicester: Inter-Varsity Press, 1983), 133–47; Léon Epsztein, *Social Justice in the Ancient Near East and the People of the Bible* (London: SCM, 1986), 45–49. I have myself discussed some aspects of it in the book of Isaiah in *Variations on a Theme: King, Messiah and Servant in the Book of Isaiah* (Carlisle: Paternoster, 1998).

6 José P. Miranda, *Marx and the Bible: A Critique of the Philosophy of Oppression* (London: SCM, 1977).

7 It may be noted in passing that Hilary Marlow uses the same word pair and several of the same texts as I do in the course of this book to draw attention to some of the ecological aspects of injustice; see 'Justice for Whom? Social and Environmental Ethics and the Hebrew Prophets', in Katharine J. Dell (ed.), *Ethical and Unethical in the Old Testament: God and Humans in Dialogue* (Library of Hebrew Bible/Old Testament Studies 528; New York: T & T Clark, 2010), 103–21.

1. The Task in Hand

> The blessing of the wretched came upon me,
>   and I caused the widow's heart to sing for joy.
> I put on *righteousness*, and it clothed me;
>   my *justice* was like a robe and a turban.
> I was eyes to the blind,
>   and feet to the lame.
> I was a father to the needy,
>   and I championed the cause of the stranger.[8]
>   (Job 29:12–16)

Similarly, if more briefly, we find comparable definitions in some of the prophets. As in the passage from Job just cited, care for the alien, orphan and widow is mentioned as a typical, almost formulaic, way of characterizing what is most characteristic of 'justice and righteousness':

> If you truly act justly with another, if you do not oppress the alien, the orphan, and the widow, or shed innocent blood in this place, and if you do not go after other gods to your own hurt … (Jer. 7:5–6)

> Act with justice and righteousness, and deliver from the hand of the oppressor anyone who has been robbed. And do no wrong or violence to the alien, the orphan, and the widow, nor shed innocent blood in this place. (Jer. 22:3)

> Render true judgments, show kindness and mercy to one another; do not oppress the widow, the orphan, the alien, or the poor; and do not devise evil in your hearts against one another. (Zech. 7:9–10)

It is worth noting at this point that the reverse is also true, namely that in their oppression of the people at large the wicked are said in explanation specifically not to care for this group of the needy:

---

[8] Unless otherwise stated I have used the *New Revised Standard Version* of the Bible for all citations.

> They pour out their arrogant words;
> > all the evildoers boast.
> They crush your people, O Lord,
> > and afflict your heritage.
> They kill the widow and the stranger,
> > they murder the orphan ...   (Psalm 94:4–6[9])

while as a token of true repentance Isaiah urges his readers to

> cease to do evil,
> > learn to do good;
> seek justice,
> > rescue the oppressed,
> defend the orphan,
> > plead for the widow   (Isaiah 1:16–17[10])

In Ezekiel 18 the prophet runs through several test cases of people who may or may not have acted justly, and each time he uses our word pair to introduce the list of actions involved. Bearing in mind the particular influence that Ezekiel's family background as a priest will have had on his choice of topics, we can see that included among more narrowly cultic concerns are the same ideals as in Job, Jeremiah and Zechariah:

> If a man is righteous and does what is lawful and right (= 'justice and righteousness') — if he does not eat upon the mountains or lift up his eyes to the idols of the house of Israel, does not defile his neighbour's wife or approach a woman during her menstrual period, does not oppress anyone, but restores to the debtor his pledge, commits no robbery, gives his bread to the hungry and covers the naked with a garment, does not take advance or accrued interest, withholds his hand from iniquity, executes true justice

---

9   It should be noted that in the wider context of the Psalm our word pair occurs in verse 15.

10 God's words in the divine council in Ps. 82:1–4 are not dissimilar, and the same attributes mark the character of God in Deut. 10:18.

1. The Task in Hand

between contending parties, follows my statutes, and is careful to observe my ordinances, acting faithfully — such a one is righteous; he shall surely live, says the Lord God.

(Ezek. 18:5–9)[11]

Andrew Mein has undertaken a detailed study of this list. As part of the argument towards his conclusion that its ethical content is part of a scaling down of sin and virtue to the more domestic and/or individual level appropriate to exile he emphasizes that the lists 'contain a typically Ezekielian mixture of religious and social injunctions, but are for the most part concerned with family and business morality'.[12]

Another argument that helps strengthen the case is to observe that in later times, after the Old Testament period, the pair changed from 'justice and righteousness' to 'justice and kindness',[13] a combination that underlines the more humanitarian as opposed to purely judicial sense of the phrase.[14] What has not been noted so often, however, is that this combination appears already within the Old Testament, all three words appearing together in a single verse at, for instance, Isa. 16:5; Jer. 9:24; Ps. 33:5; 89:14.[15] This shows that the later usage is really just an abbreviation of a longer form

---

11 There are variations on this list in verses 10–13 and 14–17, but not in ways that are significant for our purposes.

12 Andrew Mein, *Ezekiel and the Ethics of Exile* (Oxford: Oxford University Press, 2001), 190–202.

13 The Hebrew word is *chesed*, which is often translated 'loving kindness' in English versions of the Bible.

14 For references in Ecclesiasticus, some of the Dead Sea Scrolls and rabbinic literature, see Weinfeld, *Social Justice*, 19.

15 The point has, however, been taken into account by Gordon Wong, 'Random Reflections on Law and Justice in the Bible', in Daniel K. S. Koh and Kiem-Kiok Kaw (eds.), *Issues of Law and Justice in Singapore: Some Christian Reflections* (Singapore: Genesis Books and Trinity Theological College, 2009), 35–50 (47–49). More broadly, see Richard H. Hiers, *Justice and Compassion in Biblical Law* (New York: Continuum, 2009), 173–211.

of our phrase, so that the addition of the word '(loving)-kindness' is only a clarification of the meaning of the term, not a change in its meaning.

Finally, it ought to be mentioned that in the longer lived language of Mesopotamia the divine order was expressed by the Akkadian word pair *kittum-mīšarum*, 'firmness-equity', and that these became ideal characteristics of the king as well. They too were associated with social kindness.[16] The first of these words came to be represented in northwest Semitic languages as forms of *tsdq*, while the second is the equivalent of the Hebrew word for 'equity'. This too is found a number of times in connection with our words in the Old Testament, and several of the passages will be discussed more fully in later chapters of this book.[17] Apparently Hebrew *mishpat* was added to *tsedaqah* to become the standard word pair in the Hebrew Bible, though it is encouraging to see the earlier *meysharim* still retained with them from time to time.[18] This too supports the view that all this was standard vocabulary for social justice.

The nub of the problem

So far I have made a preliminary case for the view that when we read of 'justice and righteousness' in the Old Testament we should think primarily of social justice. We have also seen that quite often certain typical examples of situations where social justice is necessary (in the care of aliens, orphans and widows in

---

16 See Weinfeld, *Social Justice*, 9–12, 29–30; Richard G. Smith, *The Fate of Justice and Righteousness During David's Reign: Narrative Ethics and Rereading the Court History According to 2 Samuel 8:15–20:26* (Library of Hebrew Bible/Old Testament Studies 508; New York: T & T Clark, 2009), 42–64. For wider considerations see J. Nicholas Postgate, 'Royal Exercise of Justice Under the Assyrian Empire', in his *The Land of Assur and the Yoke of Assur: Studies on Assyria 1971–2005* (Oxford: Oxbow Books, 2007), 47–56.
17 See, for instance, Isa. 11:4; 33:15; 45:19; Ps. 9:8; 45:6–7; 58:1; 98:9; 99:4; Prov. 1:3; 2:9.
18 For comparable occurrences in Ugaritic and Phoenician, see Weinfeld, *Social Justice*, 25–26.

1. The Task in Hand

that form of society) are listed almost as stock phrases in order to make the point. That leaves open the possibility that more might be expected to be involved, but we are not always told what.

The first occurrence of our pair of words together in the Bible is instructive in this regard. In Genesis 18 there is the puzzling story of how Abraham once entertained three men in his tent and how, after some discussion about his wife Sarah, Abraham set off with them when they decided to leave in order to move in the direction of Sodom. At that point in some way that is not explained, the story progresses on the basis of Abraham conversing with God alone.[19]

God meditates on the desirability of his letting Abraham know what he is planning to do next because Abraham has been chosen to become a great nation and one through whom all the other nations will come into blessing. And God continues: 'I have chosen him, that he may charge his children and his household after him to keep the way of the Lord by doing righteousness and justice; so that the Lord may bring about for Abraham what he has promised him' (Gen. 18:19).

There is no immediate explanation of what 'doing righteousness and justice' means here, and so it would be wise not to be too restrictive. Gordon McConville, for instance, expounds it primarily in line with political considerations.[20] Nevertheless, there are some clear indications in the wider passage that concerns close to what we should call social justice are also in view.

First, this is what we should automatically expect in view of our familiarity with the phrase from elsewhere in the Bible, and no doubt this will have been presupposed by the present author.

---

19 On this passage as a whole, see, in addition to the commentaries, James K. Bruckner, *Implied Law in the Abraham Narrative: A Literary and Theological Analysis* (Journal for the Study of the Old Testament, Supplement Series 335; London: Sheffield Academic Press, 2001).

20 J. Gordon McConville, *God and Earthly Power: An Old Testament Political Theology, Genesis–Kings* (Library of Hebrew Bible/Old Testament Studies 454; London: T & T Clark, 2006), 44–46.

Second, the immediate continuation of God's soliloquy links his words closely with the sin of Sodom and Gomorrah: 'How great is the outcry against Sodom and Gomorrah and how very grave their sin! I must go down and see whether they have done altogether according to the outcry that has come to me; and if not, I will know' (Gen. 18:20–21). While the sin is again not further specified, Abraham's intercession that follows gives us a pointer by drawing a contrast between 'the righteous' and 'the wicked', and this in turn may be said to be illustrated by the story in the first part of chapter 19 which is based on proper attitudes towards hospitality towards strangers, something which we saw was fundamental to the definition of social justice within Old Testament terminology.

Third, Abraham's intercession seems further to play on God's purposes for his family when he says, 'Far be it from you to do such a thing, to slay the righteous with the wicked, so that the righteous fare as the wicked! Far be that from you! Shall not the Judge of all the earth do what is just?' (Gen. 18:25) With use of the same vocabulary as God had used concerning Abraham's family, this implies that within the fold of justice and righteousness there is an element of proportionality (we might almost say fairness) in which righteousness exceeds wickedness in effectiveness. Given the wider context of the story, it is clear that this is pitting some quality against a rigorous and narrowly legalistic understanding.

It looks, therefore, as though God wants Abraham's family to imitate him in his own concern for righteousness and justice. It starts by attending to the 'outcry' (verses 20–21; 19:13[21]) of the oppressed people in the cities — a word which is certainly related to social abuse elsewhere (e.g. Exod. 3:7; 1 Sam. 9:16; Isa. 5:7; Neh. 5:1; Prov. 21:13) — and includes movement to investigate the nature of the trouble and then quasi-judicial action to remove the evil. In principle, all that could be imitated in the human realm.

---

21 Two closely related words for 'outcry' are used in these three verses, but as it amounts to little more than a variation in spelling it is difficult to think that there is any significance in the difference.

1. The Task in Hand

But what we are not told is how we should know what constitutes 'righteousness and justice' in the first place. We may well think that the sin of Sodom and Gomorrah as depicted in Genesis 19 is obvious enough not to need further discussion, but that hardly satisfies the question at issue. If Abraham is to 'charge his children and his household after him to keep the way of the Lord by doing righteousness and justice', we might suppose that further guidance would be helpful, for more than just such outrageous behaviour as that of the two cities seems to be in view. Again, a reply might be that it means a simple imitation of God's way ('to keep the way of the Lord'), but it is easier said than done to specify exactly what that entails.

So the nub of the problem is to track down what we can of how the Old Testament expects its readers to know what is included in the fifty or more appearances of the word-pair 'justice and righteousness'.

2

Divine Justice and Natural Justice

In the first chapter I set out the nature of the problem that we are trying to answer. In the three chapters that follow this present one, I shall be looking at a number of specific Old Testament passages that may help us move towards an answer. Before I can do that, however, there are several other relevant topics that need to be considered. Israel did not live in a vacuum, for instance, so that we need to ask whether they shared, and perhaps even borrowed, some of their ideas of social justice from their neighbours; if so, we should need to take that into account when dealing with particular passages. Again, as I mentioned before, the Old Testament was written over a long period of time and in very changing political and social circumstances; how should we factor that into our investigation?

It follows from this that an early part of our task must be to make matters seem more complicated than we initially thought. But life is like that. It will not help us get to grips with one of the major topics for which we look to the Bible for guidance, namely how to live according to 'the way of the Lord by doing righteousness and justice', if we oversimplify and are not faithful both to the complexities of real life in this world and to the nature of the biblical evidence to which we look for help.

2. Divine Justice and Natural Justice

This I propose to do in four ways: first, to indicate the extent to which some of the issues which we think of as distinctively biblical were in fact shared by Israel's neighbours, including those much earlier than her, so that we can learn to appreciate how much that we regard as the fundamental concerns of justice were not peculiarly Israelite at all but rather the result of much humane as well as pragmatic thinking in the ancient world; to that extent, in other words, we need to accept the biblical validation of what we might call natural justice. In order to clarify right at the outset, I should perhaps spell out that in using the language of natural justice and the like in this book, I am not doing so in the strict medieval sense, as though knowledge of this form of justice were a wholly independent and human process of deduction without any reference to divine inspiration or knowledge of sacred history. As I hope will quickly be apparent to any reader, my position is rather that Scripture itself seems to point us to the use of reason informed by these other considerations (as known to us now primarily from the Bible itself) as a means of access to what its writers mean by 'justice and righteousness'. I have found that some older words of Henry Gehman put the point rather well: 'Although the Old Testament contains all the elements of what is regarded as natural law, we cannot go to it as a source of natural law. In the Old Testament all law is regarded as having its origin in God; this book does not reason in naturalistic terms. ... The law of God as expressed in the Old Testament includes natural law, but it also transcends it.'[1]

Second, I shall try to show that there are parts of the Old Testament which we often appeal to as most trenchantly scriptural which in fact rely precisely on an appreciation of this sense of shared values.

---

1 Henry S. Gehman, 'Natural Law and the Old Testament', in Jacob M. Myers et al. (eds.), *Biblical Studies in Memory of H. C. Alleman* (Locust Valley, NY: J. J. Augustin, 1960), 109–22.

Third, I shall supply a few examples both from within and beyond the Old Testament where we can see or suspect that changing historical and political circumstances have led to changed manners of application of given principles, thereby teaching us that it would be unwise either to lump all the material together in a single package or to draw far-reaching consequences from comparisons with other nations without attending carefully to the varying circumstances in which the passage under discussion was written.

And finally I shall give some preliminary indication of the extent to which it may be necessary to be more sensitive to the different levels within a class society which may be in view in some of the biblical exhortations, so indicating once again that not all the seemingly relevant material should automatically be lumped together as addressing the same sorts of situation.

Concerns for justice in the ancient Near East

A full survey of relevant ancient Near Eastern material is obviously out of the question. In what follows I shall merely select a few illustrative highlights in order to indicate the widespread nature of some shared values that are relevant to our present concern. In order to give the survey focus, I shall limit it in the main to references to the care of the orphan and widow. As we saw in the first chapter, this is something that is more or less stereotypical of concern for social justice in the Old Testament. As we shall discover, the same is true elsewhere, so that it is unlikely that we are dealing with things that are unrelated.

Set against the many centuries of Bible interpretation, these are all relatively recent discoveries, so that inevitably we are privileged to enjoy a fuller knowledge of the world from which the Bible came than most of our predecessors. At the same time, however, it should also be appreciated that even this new knowledge is but a drop in a bucket when compared with what we do not know; of many of Israel's closest and culturally most nearly related neighbours, such as the transjordanian states, we know next to nothing in this regard, and even for those for which we are better informed the limitations remain obvious. It is important that we remain cautious, therefore, in drawing too rigid conclusions.[2]

(1) Ugarit

I start with the kingdom of Ugarit, situated on the coast of modern Syria, because of those for which we have reasonable documentation it is in many ways the closest to ancient Israel. Reaching us from the fourteenth century B.C., its texts clearly pre-date the Israel known to us from the Old Testament. At the same time, however, they share many cultural and religious features that make them similar to the Canaanite antecedents of Israel. These had a profound influence on much that we think of as biblical, whether by assimilation, adaptation or rejection and counter-effect. The streams of tradition that they attest will have flowed also into the city-states of Canaan, and whether in Jerusalem or elsewhere it would have been impossible for the ruling circles in Israel to be unaware of them in some shape or form. Not surprisingly, therefore, we read some passages descriptive of the kings and their failures that sound quite familiar in tone to a Bible reader.

---

[2] For a much wider presentation, see Enrique Nardoni, *Rise Up, O Judge: A Study of Justice in the Biblical World* (Peabody, Massachusetts: Hendrickson Publishers, 2004), 1–41, Weinfeld; *Social Justice*; for other, briefer surveys, see Epsztein, *Social Justice*, 3–42; Bruce V. Malchow, *Social Social Justice in the Hebrew Bible: What Is New and What Is Old?* (Collegeville, MN: Liturgical Press, 1996), 1–5. The specific topic of orphans and widows was surveyed some time ago by F. Charles Fensham, 'Widow, Orphan, and the Poor in Ancient Near Eastern Legal and Wisdom Literature', *Journal of Near Eastern Studies* 21 (1962), 129–39.

In one extensive epic we read of King Keret (or Kirta).[3] Near its end we read how his son wants to succeed him and how he complains of some of his father's failures:

> Listen, noble Kirta,
> > listen closely and tend (your) ear:
>
> When raiders lead raids,
> > and creditors detain (debtors),
>
> You let your hands fall slack:
> > you do not judge the widow's case,
> > you do not make a decision regarding the oppressed,
> > you do not cast out those who prey upon the poor.
>
> Before you, you do not feed the orphan,
> > behind your back the widow. (*CoS* 1:342)

Similarly, in the course of the legend of Aqhat ('Aqhatu), we read how his father King Danilu went about his royal duties on an important day in the narrative:

> [He] arose and sat at the entrance to the (city-)gate,
> > among the leaders sitting at the threshing floor.
>
> He judged the widow's case,
> > made decisions regarding the orphan.
> > > (*CoS* 1:346, and cf. 351)

The narrative setting of each of these passages makes clear that concern for the orphan and widow is being cited as an obvious and stereotypical example of what a 'good' king should do. The nature of what is done on their behalf is not specified and in fact is not important. It is obvious — and the more extended list

---

3 For convenience, wherever possible I cite the translations offered by a wide range of experts in the three-volumed William W. Hallo and K. Lawson Younger (eds.), *The Context of Scripture* (Leiden: Brill, 1997-2002), henceforth *CoS*. Full references to other translations may be found listed there. Needless to say, there are passages where the rendering may be uncertain, as the notes to the translations indicate, but these do not generally affect the main points that I am seeking to draw from them.

2. Divine Justice and Natural Justice

in the first passage fully supports this — that they are referred to simply as the most deprived and defenceless in society and that it is therefore incumbent upon the most powerful judicial administrator to take up their cause in the absence of any other male figure to do so. The widow and orphan apparently play this part because of their lack of legal standing by virtue of land tenure or the like. It would be a mistake, therefore, immediately to extrapolate to a conclusion regarding appropriate treatment of other members of society; rather, the language is that of a cipher which we need to learn to read. The fact that we also find it regularly repeated elsewhere as well as in the Old Testament reinforces this conclusion.

(2) Mesopotamia

The literature from ancient Babylon and Assyria is more plentiful than that from Ugarit by far and it extends over many centuries both before and during the biblical period. Examples of material relevant to our theme are therefore far more numerous and only a few can be cited.

By no means the earliest, but important because the number of times it was copied indicates that it achieved something approaching canonical status, was the law-code of Hammurabi (eighteenth century B.C.). A number of the laws it includes, familiar to us also from other codes, not least in the Old Testament, relate to incidents that must have been of rare occurrence, while other topics that one might have assumed would be included are not found there. This suggests that the code was more paradigmatic than strictly functional, and its use as a school exercise for as much as a millennium after it was first written supports this suggestion.

Noteworthy, therefore, is the material included in the prologue and epilogue which sets out some of the guiding principles as understood and so promulgated by the author: at the start, Hammurabi introduces himself as the one named by the gods 'to make justice prevail in the land, to abolish the wicked and the evil, to prevent the strong from oppressing the weak ...' (*CoS* 2:336), indicating, therefore, that justice finds its first expression in the defence of those who cannot defend themselves against oppression. And in the epilogue, as part of the illustration of who that class might be, we find him giving the rationale for the erection of the stele: 'In order that the mighty not wrong the weak, to provide just ways for the waif (= orphan) and widow, I have inscribed my precious pronouncements upon my stela and set it up before the statue of me, the king of justice ... to provide just ways for the wronged' (*CoS* 2:351). It is interesting to note, therefore, how this concern is seen to undergird the whole of the legal system, even though many of the individual laws certainly relate primarily to those in more privileged positions.

Similar examples can be found in both earlier and later law codes, so indicating that this was a standard element. The earliest known to us at present comes in an account of the legal reforms of Uru-inimgina (or Uru-kagina) of Lagash (*c.* 2570–2342 B.C.), where it is stated that he 'made a compact with the divine Nin-Girsu that the powerful man would not oppress the orphan (or) widow' (*CoS* 2:408). Likewise, in the prologue to the laws of Ur-namma (or his son Shulgi), dated to the end of the third millennium B.C., we find it stated: 'I did not deliver the orphan to the rich. I did not deliver the widow to the mighty. I did not deliver the man with but one shekel to the man with one mina (i.e. 60 shekels)' (*CoS* 2:409)

Fully in line with this conclusion we find the same combination in other contexts where the aim is to extol the virtues of a good ruler. Thus, for instance, towards the end of the late third millennium, in the Cylinders of Gudea, written in Sumerian as some sort of (possibly hymnic) commemoration or dedication of a temple-building project by Gudea, king of Lagash, it is claimed that 'he had everything function as it should in his city'.[4] What this entails in then spelt out, including that:

---

4   This is the rendering of line 1211 in the Oxford University Electronic Text Corpus of Sumerian Literature.

> He did not deliver the orphan up to the rich man;
> he did not deliver up the widow to the powerful man.
> In the house that had no male heir,
> he installed the daughter as its heir.
> A day of majestic justice arose for him.

These examples are sufficient to illustrate my point that this particular element has become a formulaic means for claiming that the king is the faithful and authorized upholder of justice. Scholars may, and do, debate the extent to which any of this found practical application, but that is not the main point at issue here. The language has been turned to the purpose of propaganda and is effectively a means of gaining popular approval.

(3) Egypt

It might initially seem strange to look also towards Egypt for examples of our theme, but it should be remembered that the situation has something of a parallel with what I claimed in relation to the material from Ugarit. Just as the latter is our fullest witness to the nature of Canaanite culture in which Israel was initially at home, so too we should recall that Egypt was the prevailing power in the region for much of the second millennium B.C. In the second half of that millennium in particular, we have information from the Amarna letters about the way in which the major, though petty, powers in the land were the kings of city states who owed allegiance to the Pharaoh and who frequently appealed to him for assistance. The probability must be that many of the institutions of government were influenced by, if not borrowed from, Egypt, and it was these that in the early Iron Age the emergent Israel inherited by one means or another. We know of close parallels with Egyptian sources in connection with some of the wisdom literature, such as Proverbs. The possibility of similar influence in the realm of justice has been less frequently explored, but it is at least entirely reasonable to look.

A further problem that confronts us, however, is that we do not have law codes from ancient Egypt in the way that we do from Mesopotamia or from Israel. It is therefore not possible to make an exact like-for-like comparison but rather we have to deduce from other kinds of literature what the ideal in this regard was thought to have been. Our best guide is the wisdom or instruction literature, which lays down principles for those in training for high office.

The Instruction of Merikare — a legacy by an elderly king to his son and successor — is a text which is by no means disrespectful to the wealthy and the upper classes. Alongside that, however, and with an interesting juxtaposition of elements that we might at first consider opposed, we find the following encouragement to do justice:

> Do justice, then you endure on earth;
> Calm the weeper, don't oppress the widow,
> Don't expel a man from his father's property [i.e. an orphan],
> Don't reduce the nobles in their possessions.   (*CoS* 1:62)

In the text of Amenemhet the king apparently addresses his son about how he escaped an attempted regicide. Many scholars, however, think that it was written after his assassination by a royal scribe. Whatever the truth of the matter, we have here the voice of one who is embittered by his treatment, and this is heightened by his recall of how he had tried to live up to the highest standards expected:

> I gave to the beggar, I raised the orphan,
> I gave success to the poor as to the wealthy;
> But he who ate my food raised opposition,
> He whom I gave my trust used it to plot.   (*CoS* 1:67)

It is evident, therefore, that care for the disadvantaged as much as the wealthy was expected to gain favour with the people, rather as we saw in Mesopotamia.

The Instruction of Amenemope has close parallels in Proverbs 22–23; quite how that has come about is uncertain, but at a minimum we may say that they are clearly standing together in the

2. Divine Justice and Natural Justice

same stream of tradition, if not closer.[5] It is mainly a list of advice for an official in training, but the figure of the widow appears twice in the context of exemplifying acceptable behaviour:

> Do not move the markers of the borders of fields
> …
> Nor encroach on the boundaries of a widow

(compare Prov. 23:10: 'Do not remove an ancient landmark, or encroach on the field of orphans', and cf. 22:28[6]) and:

> Do not pounce on a widow when you find her in the fields
> And then fail to be patient with her reply.

While not as prominent as in Mesopotamia or Ugarit, these examples from Egypt are sufficient to reinforce the general conclusion that I wish to draw at this point, namely that there are many aspects relating to what we call social justice in the Old Testament, of which I have used only a standard one here as an example, which find parallels widely known also

---

5 Most modern commentaries discuss this in some detail; see, for instance, Roland E. Murphy, *Proverbs* (Word Biblical Commentary 22; Nashville: Thomas Nelson, 1998), 290–94. There is a survey of the debate about all this in R. Norman Whybray, *The Book of Proverbs: A Survey of Modern Study* (Leiden: Brill, 1995), 6–16, 78–84; in this and some other publications Whybray changed his mind about the likelihood of direct dependence of Proverbs on Amenemope; there are complementary responses to this by John A. Emerton, 'The Teaching of Amenemope and Proverbs xxii 17–xxiv 22: Further Reflections on a Long-Standing Problem', *Vetus Testamentum* 51 (2001), 431–65, and Nili Shupak, 'The Instruction of Amenemope and Proverbs 22:17–24:22 from the Perspective of Contemporary Research', in Ronald L. Troxel, Kelvin G. Friebel and Dennis R. Magary (eds.), *Seeking Out the Wisdom of the Ancients: Essays Offered to Honor Michael V. Fox on the Occasion of his Sixty-Fifth Birthday* (Winona Lake, Indiana: Eisenbrauns, 2005), 203–20.

6 Concern for the just maintenance of boundaries is also reflected elsewhere in the ancient Near East; for details, see David L. Baker, *Tight Fists or Open Hands? Wealth and Poverty in Old Testament Law* (Grand Rapids, Michigan: Eerdmans, 2009), 97–102.

elsewhere in the ancient Near East.[7] (Examples from some other regions, such as Phoenicia, could also have been added.) Furthermore, they are often earlier than the biblical literature, so that if either is the borrower it must be the latter. That does not deny them their importance, of course, but it does teach us to ponder more carefully the source for the authority of the biblical teachings. Expressions such as natural theology and natural justice have been unpopular in many Christian circles during the past century, but as we shall see in the next section of this chapter there is evidence that this imbalance is now rapidly being redressed. It will become important for us to take this point fully into account when we move later towards thinking through the issue how the ancient injunctions of scripture, which come from a culture and an age so very remote from our own, might nevertheless be able to impinge upon our own thinking about living in a just manner.

Old Testament acknowledgment of natural justice

Christians with a high view of scripture think instinctively that there is a problem both with natural theology and with natural law that may go along with it. The preacher's use of

---

[7] The case has sometimes been made that the biblical laws on care for the orphan, widow and stranger were in fact framed by the privileged elite in order to promote their own interests; cf. Mark R. Sneed, 'Israelite Concern for the Alien, Orphan, and Widow: Altruism or Ideology?', *Zeitschrift für die alttestamentliche Wissenschaft* 111 (1999), 498-507, and Harold V. Bennett, *Injustice Made Legal: Deuteronomic Law and the Plight of Widows, Strangers, and Orphans in Ancient Israel* (Grand Rapids, Michigan: Eerdmans, 2002). For responses to this position (which contains elements of truth but which is misguided in its conclusions), see Bernard S. Jackson, 'Revolution in Biblical Law: Some Reflections on the Role of Theory in Methodology', *Journal of Semitic Studies* 50 (2005), 83–115 (esp. 99–108), and more briefly Baker, *Tight Fists or Open Hands?*, who draws helpfully on Christiana van Houten, *The Alien in Israelite Law* (*Journal for the Study of the Old Testament*, Supplement Series 107; Sheffield: Sheffield Academic Press, 1991).

2. Divine Justice and Natural Justice

the expression 'the Bible says' implies on the face of it a commitment to the view that the words written were inspired by God in some way, so that there is no need to appeal to any other source for their validity.

A moment's further reflection should make clear, however, that the consequence need not follow from the basic proposition. Unless one's view of the inspiration of the Bible is one of divine dictation (which mine is not, and nor is that of the majority of believers), it is clear that the writers must have derived their material from a wide variety of sources (as, indeed, they explicitly acknowledge from time to time), so that the process of inspiration has to be seen as much broader than initially thought. A doctrine of incarnation affirms not that the divine and human are totally opposite and contrary spheres but rather that the one may work flawlessly through the other. There is thus no impediment in principle to probing the possible sources of the texts and the elements which make them up, and within the providence of God there is thus equally no objection to being open to the possibility that he used rational human processes to arrive at truth.

That both the Old and the New Testaments in fact include material which fits comfortably into this category was one of the main arguments in James Barr's 1991 Gifford Lectures,[8] and there is no need for me to go over the ground again here. What is important to note in particular, however, is the further step, which Barr discussed more briefly but which has been amplified by others both before and since, that some, if not much, of the moral and ethical instruction in the Bible is not derived either literally or metaphorically from Mount Sinai but from elsewhere. In some cases, such as much of the instruction literature in Proverbs, for instance, the origin may be very ancient — the distillation of generations of patient

---

8   James Barr, *Biblical Faith and Natural Theology: The Gifford Lectures for 1991 Delivered in the University of Edinburgh* (Oxford: Clarendon Press, 1993).

learning from experience and observation; in other cases, as we have already seen earlier, we must reckon with the likelihood that some shared values were inherited as part of a cultural given from neighbouring related peoples, adapted, no doubt, to local circumstances and norms, which of course derive in part from Israel's theology which was developed on the basis of her experience of God and his work in her world; and in yet other cases, I should wish here to maintain, there is a difficulty in finding any particular external source other than a basic humane instinct for what in broad terms may be considered right or wrong.

This comes to light especially in some of the early prophets, and in fact the tenor of their argument seems to depend upon it. When Amos, for instance, condemns some of Israel's neighbours for their conduct in war and related activities, we know that the main part of his purpose is to build up his rhetoric as he then moves in on Israel itself to utter a condemnation every bit as scathing as that which his listeners or readers, we may suppose, were approving of when uttered against their enemies. But that does not empty the earlier invective of its force. And if we ask on what basis he expected those nations to know that they were doing wrong, he does not say explicitly but he seems to assume that they were expected to be aware of it. Some of the options have been collected and analysed by John Barton.[9]

One thing at least is clear — Amos did not base himself here directly on any biblical law; he does not cite any and of course it would have been unreasonable to expect foreign nations to have been aware of them. A few scholars have argued that there is an appeal here back to some sense of solidarity among these

---

9 John Barton *Amos's Oracles against the Nations: A Study of Amos 1.3–2.5* (The Society for Old Testament Study Monograph Series 6; Cambridge: Cambridge University Press, 1980), reprinted in *Understanding Old Testament Ethics: Approaches and Explorations* (Louisville, KY: Westminster John Knox, 2003), 77–129.

nations in relation to Israel by virtue of the old Davidic empire,[10] but apart from the historical uncertainties upon which this theory is based it is difficult to understand how that could apply as late as the eighth century, and in particular, in any case, not all the crimes cited are directed against Israel in the first place.

Rather, against these and similar notions, Barton makes the case that the nations are guilty of transgressing against what he calls 'international customary law', which he goes on to explain more fully: 'These conventions are called customary because they are clearly not the subject of explicit legislation, and "international" because they are concerned with conduct between independent nations in time of war'. But if these conventions were not explicitly laid down (though Barton seeks to give evidence to suggest that they were recognized by other nations in some shape or form), then they effectively become part of what I have called natural justice, i.e. that there are certain forms of behaviour which are simply unacceptable — and of course part of Amos's purpose is startlingly and apparently for the first time to put Israel's infringement of the principles of social justice on the same level. In his further discussion Barton makes clear that he is effectively saying the same thing: 'our point is that he is appealing not to revealed law, but to conventional or customary law'.

My only addition to this well-argued case is to suggest that the link with the following sayings against Israel in the next chapters is not only to see a parallel being made with transgressions against social law but also that the punishment adumbrates what is also new in Amos's message, namely that the whole nation is to come under judgment, not just the individual transgressors. What strikes me as being the particularly pointed nature of his condemnation of other nations is not just that they have done something horrible,

---

10 See, for instance, John Mauchline, 'Implicit Signs of a Persistent Belief in the Davidic Empire', *Vetus Testamentum* 20 (1970), 287–303, and Max E. Polley, *Amos and the Davidic Empire: A Socio-Historical Approach* (New York: Oxford University Press, 1989), 55–82.

but that they in fact went further than anyone would expect even within the naturally horrific cruelties of war: for instance, that seems to be the force of the metaphorical statement in the first oracle, against Damascus, that 'they have threshed Gilead with threshing-sledges of iron' (1:3), clearly depicting mistreatment of the whole population rather than just the military. In the case of Gaza, 'they carried into exile entire communities, to hand them over to Edom' (1:6; this is echoed in the following, probably secondary, oracle against Tyre, 1:9), rather than those actually involved in the conflict. Ammon's condemnation is similar in that they 'ripped open pregnant women in Gilead' (1:13), illustrative of the most obviously non-combatant elements of the population; and so on. And if this is right, it would perhaps fit well with Amos's later message in his sayings and visions, where for the first time it is the judgment on Israel as a whole, rather than just kings or other individuals, which is the new element in his message.

Whether or not this last suggestion is correct, the important point for our present purpose is the recognition that Amos here appeals not to some law of God revealed overtly in scripture or elsewhere but to a sense of common decency at however basic a level which he can reasonably expect to be shared by all the peoples, not just by Israel. The argument of his prophecy simply will not work without it.[11]

Indications of development or change

Because the Old Testament has been preserved as the scripture of two live religions, readers over the centuries have devised all sorts of strategies, some better justified than others, for handling it as some sort of a unity. This reading process, however, should not be confused with or used as an excuse to avoid acknowledging the very real evidence for differences between the parts that are

---

11 This, and its wider implications for our subject as a whole, has been expressed much better than I could ever manage in John Barton, *Ethics and the Old Testament* (London: SCM, 1998), especially 58–76.

most naturally explained as a consequence of the long period of time during which it was written. And an important element of our study here is to suggest that in fact we may arrive at a more satisfactory approach to interpretation in the modern world if we follow through on this equally modern form of observation.

Among the lines of evidence that might most easily be adduced in this introductory discussion may be included as of first importance the differences between the various law codes in the Pentateuch. While many of the details remain the object of academic debate, there is no difficulty in recognizing three main codes, between which, as we shall see, there are areas of both overlap and distinction.

First, we have the so-called Book of the Covenant in Exodus 20–23 (the name derives from Exod. 24:7). Of the three codes, this is the most concise in form of expression, and the view of the overwhelming majority of scholars (which I share) is that this is the earliest of the three main codes.

Second in biblical order come the laws that are found mainly in the book of Leviticus, though with some relevant material in Numbers as well. For a variety of reasons, these laws are usually ascribed to priestly authors, and they certainly include much material of direct relevance to religious practice. Alongside that, however, there is also material of wider application. Because it is difficult to see that these laws had much influence on other biblical literature before the period of the Babylonian exile at the earliest, and most markedly even later than that, the usual view is that in its present form this code is the latest of the three. That is not to deny that it incorporates or modifies material of earlier origin, of course. Because of this, an influential minority in fact date it earlier, though I find their arguments hard to endorse in their entirety. This dispute is itself instructive for us, however. It cannot be denied that there are many uncertainties in the handling of material from so very long ago, and it is appropriate that we should acknowledge that fact. However, whichever solution we eventually favour, it does not detract from the most important consequence in our present discussion, namely that some of the laws may be laid alongside equivalent laws in the other codes and differences observed. And that itself is sufficient for our present purpose.

Finally, the (central part of the) book of Deuteronomy includes another law code, again quite easily identifiable by its distinctive language, style and ideological point of view. Most scholars have dated this at the end of the period of the Judean monarchy because of its apparently close association with the reforms that King Josiah undertook (2 Kings 22–23). Again, there are voices raised in favour of somewhat earlier and later dates, but as with the other codes the exact dating is not significant for us.

Now, as I have already indicated, there are a number of laws in these codes that are of direct relevance to the theme of social justice[12] even if our word pair as such does not occur there, and sometimes they appear in two or even three of the codes. These have often then been laid alongside one another and the differences observed. We may cite aspects of the laws relating to slaves as a standard example of this sort: see the table set out on the next page.

It is obvious that to undertake a full study of the relationship between these three passages would take far more space than can be justified here; others have done so with varying evaluations of their relative chronology, and I have no intention of getting further into that debate now.[13] It is enough for my purpose to say that anyone reading through the three passages can see that they cover the same topic but with smaller or larger differences between them. Change in the law over time, either to reflect different historical circumstances or, more likely, to reflect developing ideologies, is the obvious conclusion to draw.

---

12 For a brief survey, see, for instance, Malchow, *Social Justice*, 20–30. For a more comprehensive scholarly treatment, see Baker, *Tight Fists or Open Hands?*

13 For a recent brief survey with abundant bibliography, see Baker, *Tight Fists or Open Hands?*, 166–73.

Exodus 21:2–11	Deut. 15:12–17	Lev. 25:39–42
When you buy a male Hebrew slave, he shall serve for six years, but in the seventh he shall go out a free person, without debt. If he comes in single, he shall go out single; if he comes in married, then his wife shall go out with him. If his master gives him a wife and she bears him sons or daughters, the wife and her children shall be her master's and he shall go out alone. But if the slave declares, 'I love my master, my wife, and my children; I will not go out a free person', then his master shall bring him before God. He shall be brought to the door or the doorpost; and his master shall pierce his ear with an awl; and he shall serve him for life. When a man sells his daughter as a slave, she shall not go out as the male slaves do. If she does not please her master, who designated her for himself, then he shall let her be redeemed; he shall have no right to sell her to a foreign people, since he has dealt unfairly with her. If he designates her for his son, he shall deal with her as with a daughter. If he takes another wife to himself, he shall not diminish the food, clothing, or marital rights of the first wife. And if he does not do these three things for her, she shall go out without debt, without payment of money.	If a member of your community, whether a Hebrew man or a Hebrew woman, is sold to you and works for you for six years, in the seventh year you shall set that person free. And when you send a male slave out from you a free person, you shall not send him out empty-handed. Provide liberally out of your flock, your threshing-floor, and your wine press, thus giving to him some of the bounty with which the Lord your God has blessed you. Remember that you were a slave in the land of Egypt, and the Lord your God redeemed you; for this reason I lay this command upon you today. But if he says to you, 'I will not go out from you', then you shall take an awl and thrust it through his earlobe into the door, and he shall be your slave for ever. You shall do the same with regard to your female slave.	If any who are dependent on you become so impoverished that they sell themselves to you, you shall not make them serve as slaves. They shall remain with you as hired or bound labourers. They shall serve with you until the year of the jubilee. Then they and their children with them shall be free from your authority; they shall go back to their own family and return to their ancestral property. For they are my servants, whom I brought out of the land of Egypt; they shall not be sold as slaves are sold...

Another area where we must suppose that there was change over time concerns land tenure. This is a topic to which we shall need to return later, as there have been important developments in our understanding in the recent past, but it is clearly most unlikely that the apportionment of land will have remained static between the pre-monarchical period, the situation under a native Israelite or Judean monarch and in the post-exilic period, when Judah was a modest province within the wider Persian empire. Changes in customary law as well as in internal development of estates and the like and later external imperial demands will all have had a bearing on this topic. And yet some scholars who have written on the topic of social justice in the past have presented data from different periods as though the social and legal situation remained static over hundreds of years. Once again, we need to be more finely attuned to the different contexts within which similar sounding language may have been invoked.

Finally by way of illustration under this heading I should like to point to the recent study by Crouch on ethical thought about warfare, who draws attention to a significant development over a modest period of time in this regard.[14]

This is an important point that is also too frequently ignored when biblical material is compared to that of Israel's ancient neighbours. Scholars tend to compare whatever they can find that may seem to resemble the biblical text without considering whether there is what we might call a chronological match. In an earlier section of this chapter, we drew on material of an exceptionally wide span of time in order to justify the suggestion that some repeated elements must have become stereotypical or formulaic. At a narrower level of application, however, it is clear that we must not lose sight of the fact that Israel's neighbours were every bit as

---

14 Carly L. Crouch, *War and Ethics in the Ancient Near East: Military Violence in Light of Cosmology and History* (Beihefte zur *Zeitschrift für die alttestamentliche Wissenschaft* 407; Berlin: de Gruyter, 2009).

much changing societies as was Israel, so that comparisons need to be considered with particular care and attention paid to the consequences of that realization.

In sum, exegesis that is historically sensitive and alert should further dissuade us from quickly lumping together everything that is superficially similar. As we have seen from other considerations, variety in the biblical sources is to be prized and embraced.

Class distinctions within ancient Israelite society

The last point that needs to be stressed in this introductory survey can be made quite briefly, but it is another that should have an important bearing on our examination of the biblical texts relating to social justice.

A number of the books that have treated this theme before give the impression that ancient Israelite society was divided neatly into two: the rich and the poor. While some parts of the Old Testament, such as many of the Proverbs, might be thought to adopt the standpoint of the rich, most affirm that the predominant view of the writers is to uphold the rights of the poor against the rich, who are judged as immoral oppressors.

This sharp dichotomizing is too simplistic, however, and it rather ignores the very different social structures of Israel from those that prevail in the modern world. In my opinion there is no escaping the conclusion that both ideally and in practice society was hierarchically ordered, and although of course there can be (and is) much criticism of individuals at any level of the social pile, there is little evidence to suggest that the whole structure should be overturned. Rather, whatever abuses the later medieval feudal structure may have nurtured, in Israel the emphasis was upon the ideal that superior status implied enhanced responsibility to those lower down, and indeed we often find that the well-being of nation and society is thought to have been dependent in rather a direct manner on the faithfulness of the king or other leaders.

We shall return later on to consider some of the evidence for this view and its implications in more detail. At this point, however, it needs to be stressed that economic dependence by many in the texts is not itself to be seen as unusual or even undesirable.[15] Just as in a family wife and children will have been dependent in many respects upon the dominant male in a manner that might raise eyebrows today, so nuclear families were in a wider relationship with extended families and/or village communities, which in turn will have had their own levels of support structures.[16] Equally, we may ascend higher up the scale and see comparable networks which require sympathetic examination in order to see how, in fact, they worked to maintain the survival of the nation through significant periods of ups and downs. To read some histories of prophetic literature, for instance, one might gain the impression that there was an economic crisis that endured for at least three hundred years! But if that contradiction in terms is an obvious absurdity, it is clear that we need to read the same material with fresh eyes.

In making this point, I have no wish to deny that from time to time — and perhaps more frequently than was in any way acceptable — there were some who were genuinely destitute. Why, and what should be done about them, is an important

---

15 This apparently simple statement hides the very real difficulties we now have in accurately characterizing the nature of the society of the Biblical communities. Four models are fully and carefully presented and analysed by Walter J. Houston, *Contending for Justice: Ideologies and Theologies of Social Justice in the Old Testament* (Library of Hebrew Bible/Old Testament Studies 428; London: T & T Clark, 2006), 18–51 (rent capitalism, 'ancient' class society, tributary state, and patronage system). While he picks and chooses as best he can among these, the one firm conclusion that he reaches, and that we need to bear in mind in our own handling of these texts, is that 'nothing in the range of social relationships canvassed in this account bears the least structural resemblance to modern capitalism' (p. 51).

16 Houston, *Justice—The Biblical Challenge*, 20–35, draws distinctions to a similar effect between village, state, city and religious community.

topic to consider. But for the moment I am content to leave the point at that and to urge that we do not confuse what we might call poverty within a society that is structured to deal justly with that and destitution, which the normal social structures have no mechanism to handle. As with the other topics already introduced, the significant factor to bear in mind is that things were not so simple as many books have suggested. As with literature and history, so with social structures there was more variety and complexity than we have often acknowledged. And in addressing such varied topics, the Old Testament, I have suggested, does not work in a legalistic manner, as though we could tick off our adherence to biblical standards on a checklist. Rather, what used to be called natural justice also has something to say in this realm, as I have indicated and as we shall see more fully later on.

3

The Individual and Social Justice

In the previous chapter I tried to illustrate a number of ways in which simplistic discussions about justice in the Old Testament fail to take into account several important factors which evidently make the task more complicated than we might at first have hoped. We saw that some features that we often think of as particularly biblical were in fact shared by many of Israel's neighbours, that some of these furthermore were not — indeed could not have been — directly based on God's revealed law as known from the Pentateuch, that circumstances changed so radically through the long course of ancient Israel's history that we should do the material less than justice if we tried to lump it all together as a legislated whole, and finally that we should try also to take into fuller account than hitherto the more variegated class structure of ancient Israel in its various periods.

In this chapter, I want to move on to consider what might be called the normal expectations on individual members of society in regard to social justice. We shall deal in later chapters with some of the passages in the prophets and the psalms which many consider to be peculiarly distinctive of the biblical message. More often than not, however, these relate to the king or to others in high authority. It seems more helpful to begin with the norm rather than the exception.

Who is Proverbs for?

For this purpose it seems that the most convenient starting point is the book of Proverbs. Here if anywhere we may expect to find reflections on how ordinary people should live, and moreover it is likely that the proverbs and other material gathered in this book were collected over a wide time span, so that there may be the further advantage that it reflects something of the basic assumptions of the society through much of its history about the good life. The book itself acknowledges something of this chronological spread, for it presents itself initially as the proverbs of Solomon (Prov. 1:1, 'The Proverbs of Solomon son of David, king of Israel'; see also 10:1) and then much later it refers both to a general collection of some sayings of the wise (24:23) and especially to the work of copying in the reign of Hezekiah, some 300 years or so later (Prov. 25:1, 'These are other proverbs of Solomon that the officials of King Hezekiah of Judah copied'). Finally, chapters 30 and 31 are ascribed to other rulers of uncertain origin. Modern scholars would generally go even further than this and see varying amounts of material deriving from the post-exilic period as well.

A further introductory question on which I ought to say a word is the extent to which I am justified in regarding Proverbs as reflecting standard expectations for a good life in ancient Israel. After all, the Egyptian parallels that are often cited in relation to Proverbs were most addressed either to high court administrators or sometimes even to royalty. Moreover, there is talk of the king in Proverbs, and the series of instructions in Proverbs 1–9, at least, are obviously addressed to young men who seem to be being prepared for the scribal or other high office.

In answering this question, we may note that there has been a good deal of discussion about the precise identity of those addressed in Proverbs. Some restrictive elements are unavoidable — for instance, the book is certainly addressed to men rather than directly to women. Beyond that, the social class and status of the audience is less clear. Whybray, for instance, sought to draw a distinction between those addressed in chapters 1–9 as members of the upper-class urban elite (as might be expected from what I have just written about those chapters), whereas he considered most of the rest of the book to have the standard 'middle-class' (as we might say) agricultural community primarily in view.[1] He himself terms this latter group 'persons of moderate means mainly engaged in farming their own land' (p. 114), and he notes in particular the extent to which they were conscious of the precariousness of life both in absolute terms and in that it was easy to fall into poverty if they did not continue to work hard. At the same time, they were encouraged to be generous to the genuinely poor (who have no direct voice in the book) and to remember that as often as not significant new wealth could only be obtained by dishonest or oppressive means.

This analysis has been challenged, however. In the first place, some, like David Pleins, have tried to argue that Proverbs was effectively written entirely by and for the elite, with the consequence that the values and practices which it portrays are wholly in accord with the interests of the ruling classes.[2] While it is possible to find some proverbs that seem to support this view, it has been shown by Malchow and especially Houston,[3] to go

---

[1] R. Norman Whybray, *Wealth and Poverty in the Book of Proverbs* (*Journal for the Study of the Old Testament*, Supplement Series 99; Sheffield: Sheffield Academic Press, 1990). We might note one of his introductory comments with relation to the sentence proverbs that they are 'of particular interest because it is often in such tiny nuggets of perceived "wisdom"—often called "sentence literature"—that a people's traditional attitudes are most convincingly encapsulated' (p. 9).

[2] J. David Pleins, *The Social Visions of the Hebrew Bible: A Theological Introduction* (Louisville, Kentucky: Westminster John Knox, 2001), 452–83.

[3] Malchow, *Social Justice*, 72; Walter J. Houston, 'The Role of the Poor in Proverbs', in J. Cheryl Exum and Hugh G.M. Williamson (eds.), *Reading from Right to Left: Essays on the Hebrew Bible in Honour of David J.A. Clines* (*Journal for the Study of the Old Testament*, Supplement Series 373; London: Sheffield Academic Press, 2003), 229–40.

3. The Individual and Social Justice

no further, that this is very far from doing justice to major parts of the book, and it may anyway rest upon some misconceptions about the setting of the book's writing in the first place. As with Whybray's view, it suffers from the error of being too one-sided.

It seems, therefore, that both approaches mentioned so far suffer from analysing the material in ways that may be too neat and restrictive.[4] It is observed that even in the sentence proverbs there are plenty that seem to presuppose settings other than the agricultural, and in any case there is no need to assume that only small farmers are interested in agricultural issues. Moreover, while Whybray sought to explain away the so-called court proverbs as being of general application (as with the English saying 'a cat may look at a king', which does not presuppose a court setting), some of the sayings relating to that context do not seem to be meaningful in any other setting.

My own appraisal of this debate is that it is almost certainly mistaken to try to find a single social or geographical setting for these proverbs. While the urban and elite setting of much of Proverbs 1–9 seems to be agreed, in my opinion the variety of sentence proverbs which follow should be allowed to stand. Taken on their own and based upon their content, the likelihood is that they derive from a wide variety of settings. Whybray's contribution should not be undervalued, for he certainly imposed a significant check on those who were tending simply to lump everything together in some kind of upper school setting. At the same time, he perhaps fell into the opposite trap of finding a single setting of a different sort for the same material. In fact, as is the nature of proverbial sayings, we may allow that they have been collected from a wide range of settings. Their collection and editing may well have been a more professional scribal activity, so that the book as a whole may have owed its origin as such to narrower circles within Judah, but at one end that

---

4   For a summary of the arguments of several other scholars (with whom he appears broadly to agree), see Houston, *Contending for Justice*, 117–19.

does not determine where the proverbs were collected from and at the other, given that there is generally agreed to be a certain amount (if not a great deal) of post-exilic origin in the book we now have it is clear that the later editorial stages were carried out in circles other than the court (though quite what sort of wisdom academy there may have been in Persian or Hellenistic Jerusalem is unknown to us).

Finally on this point, while I am therefore reassured in my position that we may take Proverbs as broadly indicative of the nature of ancient Israelite beliefs in what constitutes a good life, we shall also see later on that this portrayal rests upon theological principles which in fact reflect a form of thinking that would be appropriate at any social level. The precise determination of the status of the intended audience thus turns out not to be absolutely crucial for our wider purposes.

A practical problem arises at this point, however, namely, how shall we identify material that is specifically relevant to our overall subject? On the one hand, in order not to allow the discussion to get out of hand, we might hope to identify the Hebrew words which come closest in meaning to what we call social justice and to limit our attention to passages where they occur. On the other hand, it is obvious that in ancient times as today people may often speak about social justice without actually using that term explicitly, and it would be impoverishing not to use common sense to identify such passages as well (albeit selectively).

I propose, therefore, that the most secure method to adopt is to start with passages where the subject is explicit and then from that reasonably firm basis to move on to others where the vocabulary may be absent but where the content seems naturally to fit.

As I explained in the introductory chapter, social justice is most closely expressed in Hebrew by the use of two familiar words together, namely *mishpat* and *tsedaqah*, 'justice and righteousness'.

3. The Individual and Social Justice

We saw also, however, that sometimes these words could be combined with others of similar significance, and also that on other occasions the context might be enough to flag up for us the presence of the same concerns even when only one of the words was being used in its own.

Thus, just to give a simple example for the moment, the combination in Isaiah 1:21 is an obvious passage for the basic phrase:

> How the faithful city
>   has become a whore!
> She that was full of *justice*,
>   *righteousness* lodged in her — but now murderers!

The same concerns are equally clearly present, however, in a passage such as Prov. 29:7, 'The *righteous* know the rights of the poor', so that clearly we must be careful not to be overly constrained by narrow-minded technicalities.

Social Justice in Proverbs

If we now turn with these preliminaries in mind to the book of Proverbs, we find that the two words are used in combination on a number of occasions. First, and significantly, they form a prominent element in the opening statement of the purpose of the book as a whole, where it is stated that the proverbs are 'for gaining instruction in wise dealing, righteousness, justice, and equity' (1:3).[5] It is noteworthy that our two key words are here combined with a third — 'equity' — which we saw earlier was

---

5 William P. Brown, *Character in Crisis: A Fresh Approach to the Wisdom Literature of the Old Testament* (Grand Rapids, Michigan: Eerdmans, 1996), 23–30, observes that 'righteousness, justice and equity' occur as the central element of the concentrically arranged sevenfold constellation of virtues in verses 2–7. Moreover, he shows later (pp. 43–49) that, being 'rooted in specific action, on the levels of both communal structure and individual conduct', they are 'a litmus test for determining the community's character'.

the Hebrew equivalent of one of the fundamental words in the equivalent Akkadian phraseology (*mīšarum*). This serves as an additional indicator that we are looking at a key passage.

This comes in a short passage which is often called the prologue to the book, and it was probably added late in the process of composition. It is likely, therefore, that the editor knows of the use of such language elsewhere in the Old Testament, including some of the prophets, where many scholars have found a more distinctive meaning, as we shall see later in this book. That should not detract from the importance of its use here, however; it demonstrates that Proverbs was read at this late time as being compatible, at the least, with other biblical material even while many scholars have sought to drive a wedge between this book and most others. We shall certainly be seeing that Proverbs has some positions of its own to maintain on issues of social justice, but these were evidently not regarded by a late editor as being untenable alongside other biblical material. This insight from a scholar in antiquity, furthermore, should give us somewhat greater flexibility in tracing our theme even when the vocabulary may differ a little from the standard. Clearly, if the book could be read then as highlighting instruction in social justice it would seem reasonable for us to try to do the same.

This conclusion is reinforced secondly by the use of the same terms in chapter 2. The link is especially impressive because, as in chapter 1, 'equity' is added again to the standard pair. At the core of the opening chapters of Proverbs is a series of instructions from a 'father' (and occasionally also a mother) to a son (cf. 1:8; 2:1; 3:1; 4:1, 10, 20; 5:1; 6:20; 7:1). This may reflect a literal family relationship as being the primary educational setting in ancient Israel, or it may be metaphorical for a teacher/pupil relationship. Either way, the basis of these instructions is the urge to act prudently in a number of practical ways, and it is indicated several times that 'wisdom' is both the source and the goal of such behaviour, an important subject to which we shall return shortly. In chapter 2 it is stated that this wisdom comes ultimately from God, and

3. The Individual and Social Justice

its outcome is that 'then you will understand righteousness and justice and equity' (2:9). Clearly, then, the author of the prologue found that his summarizing of the book as a whole was already adumbrated in its opening instructions.

Looking further afield, and allowing that sometimes the words are used in different forms and somewhat more freely than in our first two examples, we find the following subjects mentioned. At Prov. 12:5 there is a somewhat general contrast between the righteous and the wicked: 'The thoughts of the righteous are just (literally: justice); the advice of the wicked is treacherous'. The picture in 21:15 is similar: 'When justice is done, it is a joy to the righteous, but dismay to evildoers'. This contrasting of the righteous and the wicked is extremely common in Proverbs, as we shall see, and quite often, as in these two cases, the sense is wide and general. It seems to be one of the main ways by which the authors categorize humanity. To find this common theme explicitly tied in to our concern by the use of the two words we are currently focusing on together is thus reassuring.

In Prov. 16:8 this same pairing is used in connection with wealth: 'Better is a little with righteousness than large income with injustice (literally: no justice)'. As we shall see, another significant way in which the authors categorize humanity is by the contrast between rich and poor, and frequently they seem to endorse the idealized view that the righteous end up being, or are, rich and that the wicked are or will become poor. It is thus noteworthy that in this saying wealth is shown ultimately to be inferior or subservient to the demand for righteousness. It helps us to establish a hierarchy of human values.

In a similar vein, though in relation to another sphere, Prov. 21:3 is noteworthy: 'To do righteousness and justice is more acceptable to the Lord than sacrifice'. Although the older view that Proverbs is devoid of any cultic concerns has been shown to be questionable,[6] nevertheless one is tempted to think that such

---

6 See Leo G. Perdue, *Wisdom and Cult: A Critical Analysis of the Views of Cult in the Wisdom Literature of Israel and the Ancient Near East* (Society of

a saying as this would not have been out of place among some of the more radical of the pre-exilic prophets. It links closely with what we have already seen with regard to the prologue to the book as a whole.

The legal realm is also represented in this group, even though the language here seems not to be especially concerned with social justice: 'It is not right to be partial to the guilty, or to subvert the innocent in judgment' (Prov. 18:5). The use of language here is interesting. As elsewhere, the English translation 'guilty' and 'innocent' is the same as what we have been rendering as 'wicked' and 'righteous'. This is perfectly regular and it reminds us that we must allow ways of looking at such categorizations to overlap in ways that may not be initially obvious to us. This is something that will become particularly important in our last main chapter, but it is helpful to be alerted to it already here as it will recur in several other connections as well.

Indeed, the last passage where these two Hebrew roots occur together in Proverbs brings this very point back to the centre of our major topic, for 31:9 states: 'Speak out, judge righteously (= enact righteous justice), defend the rights of the poor and needy'. This is an important collocation of ideas. We tend to think of justice and judgment as something intimidating; we associate it only with the possibility of being found guilty and so of suffering punishment. This verse, by contrast, and many others like it that we shall encounter later, indicates that justice and judgment can rather be positive — a putting to right of things that may have gone wrong. Whereas all too often the poor and needy in the modern world seem to get on the wrong side of the judicial system, here we find by contrast that the courts are their one human hope. There is thus a sense in which justice in the strictly legal sense and what we call social justice in fact overlap, bringing many of the passages that we have already listed into line with one another.

There is one more passage where our two words occur together, but before turning to that I think it would be worthwhile briefly

---

Biblical Literature Dissertation Series 30; Missoula, Montana: Scholars Press, 1977).

3. The Individual and Social Justice

to draw attention to the fact that there are many more passages where one or other of the words occurs on their own, but in expressions that come close in subject matter to the subjects we have already mentioned. These cannot all be discussed in detail, because they are so numerous, but even a short listing is important at this point because it illustrates how pervasive these matters are for the authors of the book.

General references to the contrast between the righteous and the wicked are extremely common, especially with use of words from the 'righteous' group. See, for instance, Prov. 11:19, 'Whoever is steadfast in righteousness will live, but whoever pursues evil will die', or Prov. 12:5, 'The thoughts of the righteous are just; the advice of the wicked is treacherous'.[7]

In connection with wealth, 'in the house of the righteous there is much treasure, but trouble befalls the income of the wicked' (Prov. 15:6); see also 10:2–3 (and cf. 11:4); 13:21, 25.

The legal realm is also well represented, including topics like honest testimony (Prov. 18:28, with 'justice', and 12:17 with 'righteous') and unbiased judgment (Prov. 16.23; 24:23, with 'justice', and 17:15, 26; 24:24, with 'righteous'). We should also note in this connection the authors' concerns for fair dealing with 'honest balances' and accurate weights (Prov. 16:11; cf. 11:1; 20:10, 23).

More closely aligned with issues of social justice are Prov. 13:23, 'The field of the poor may yield much food, but it is swept away through injustice (= "not justice")', and 'The righteous know the rights of the poor; the wicked have no such understanding' (Prov. 29:7).

The theological basis

I return now to the remaining passage where our two key terms occur together, Prov. 8:20. In this passage, wisdom is speaking, and she declares of herself that 'I walk in the way

---

7 Similar wide-ranging expressions occur at Prov. 10:2, 25; 11:4, 5, 6, 18; 12:28; 13:6; 14:32; 15:9; 21:18, 21; 24:16–16; 28:1, and so on.

of righteousness, along the paths of justice'. Here we find the important insight given that human action in this realm is ultimately imitative of wisdom's, and this is something that is then reflected, in my opinion, in statements made in particular about rulers and kings in Israel. For instance, just earlier in this same chapter we find wisdom asserting that 'by me kings reign, and rulers decree what is just; by me rulers rule, and nobles, all who govern rightly' (8:15–16). Similarly, 'take away the wicked from the presence of the king, and his throne will be established in righteousness' (25:5).

There has been a good deal of discussion about this aspect of 'righteousness', and in particular whether it is an Israelite equivalent of the Egyptian goddess Ma'at.[8] It has long been established that there are many connections of form and content between Proverbs and the Egyptian instruction texts, and the supposition would be that this parallel would fit with that circumstance. Ma'at's name has been rendered by some as 'order, justice, what is right, truth'. It was initially an abstract noun for divine order but became hypostatized as a goddess, and there can be no doubt that in many respects her role resembles that of 'righteousness' in Proverbs and related literature. We even

---

8   The case has been most strongly made by Hans H. Schmid, *Gerechtigkeit als Weltordnung: Hintergrund und Geschichte des alttestamentlichen Gerechtigkeitsbegriffes* (Beiträge zur Historischen Theologie 40; Tübingen: J. C. B. Mohr [Paul Siebeck], 1968). This book has not been translated into English, but one may gain access to at least some of the elements of Schmid's case in his essay 'Creation, Righteousness, and Salvation: "Creation Theology" as the Broad Horizon of Biblical Theology', in Bernhard W. Anderson (ed.), *Creation in the Old Testament* (Issues in Religion and Theology 6; Philadelphia: Fortress, and London: SPCK, 1984), 102–17. More recently the book has been described and analysed by Henning Graf Reventlow, 'Righteousness as Order of the World: Some Remarks Towards a Programme', in Henning Graf Reventlow and Yair Hoffman (eds.), *Justice and Righteousness: Biblical Themes and their Influence* (*Journal for the Study of the Old Testament*, Supplement Series 137; Sheffield: JSOT Press, 1992), 163–72.

3. The Individual and Social Justice

find, as an especially close parallel, that Pharaoh's throne can be depicted with what looks like a hieroglyph for Ma'at at its base.[9]

Whether or not we should see 'righteousness' in some verses in Proverbs as a direct borrowing from this Egyptian source or regard the two concepts only as closely parallel need not, perhaps, be decided here. Rather, the point that I should wish to draw from the suggested parallel is that even the few verses to which I drew attention at the start of this section of the chapter indicate that righteousness, and hence all that follows from it, is depicted in this book as equally a foundation principle of the world and the nature of its human rule as experienced in those ancient times. It is as the king and other rulers fit in with this explicitly acknowledged principle of wisdom that good order in society prevails. And that, it may be suggested, should then be reflected in all lower levels of society as the more powerful or wealthy deal with others lower down the order.

---

9 For an introductory summary with reference to more specialized studies, see Klaas A.D. Smelik, 'Ma'at', in Karel van der Toorn, Bob Becking and Pieter W. van der Horst (eds.), *Dictionary of Deities and Demons in the Bible* (2nd edn; Leiden: Brill and Grand Rapids, Michigan: Eerdmans, 1999), 534–35; Nardoni, *Rise Up, O Judge*, 21–41. At a more technical level, see further among many other discussions Hartmut Gese, *Lehre und Wirklichkeit in der alten Weisheit* (Tübingen: J.C.B. Mohr, 1958); R. Norman Whybray, *Wisdom in Proverbs: The Concept of Wisdom in Proverbs 1–9* (Studies in Biblical Theology 45; London: SCM, 1965), 54–56; Christa Kayatz, *Studien zu Proverbien 1–9: Eine form- und motivgeschichtliche Untersuchung unter Einbeziehung Ägyptischen Vergleichsmaterials* (Wissenschaftliche Monographien zum Alten und Neuen Testament 22; Neukirchen-Vluyn: Neukirchener Verlag, 1966), 93–139; Hans H. Schmid, *Wesen und Geschichte der Weisheit: Eine Untersuchung zur altorientalischen und israelitischen Weisheitsliteratur* (Beihefte zur Zeitschrift für die alttestamentliche Wissenschaft 101; Berlin: Alfred Töpelmann, 1966), and *Gerechtigkeit als Weltordnung*; Jan Assmann, *Ma'at: Gerechtigkeit und Unsterblichkeit im Alten Ägypten* (Munich: Beck, 1990; 2nd edn, 2006); Eckart Otto, *Theologische Ethik des Alten Testaments* (Theologische Wissenschaft 3,2; Stuttgart: Kohlhammer, 1994), 117–42.

The basis for social justice, then, becomes not an adherence to some set of written laws, nor to some arbitrary decisions of the deity or his human representatives.[10] Rather, the fundamental basis for human behaviour becomes a fitting in to the established order of the universe. The principal instructor, then, is Wisdom, whether metaphorically or, in one or two passages, personified. She lives by and exemplifies righteousness, and this should then be reflected similarly by others. This is something which can be learnt, then, by instruction from seniors or equally by observation of how things are and work. Thus many of the proverbs become, in effect, observations of the way of the world, and the good life — the wise life — is to accommodate oneself to that for the long term, even if it appears to be disadvantageous in the short term. It is, in effect, a form of natural law.

Human compliance

A few examples might help to clarify the point. Starting from chapter 10 for convenience (i.e. the first chapter of the sentence proverbs), we find as the opening proverb that 'A wise child makes a glad father, but a foolish child is a mother's grief'. Now of course the relationship of parents to children is a subject of one of the ten commandments, and there are also other passages in the law which deal with the same matter. This proverb, however, is not directly related to those, but is quite obviously the result of simple observation and is as true of any other culture as it is of Israel. No parent would be likely to deny its truth. From this observation it might then be possible to proceed to draw out some obvious common-sense consequences for behaviour by children which would lead them to have a less unhappy life in

---

10 It is striking to observe as a parallel that after his survey of the use of our word pair in the Pentateuch and main historical books McConville can summarize his findings by saying that 'the effect of beginning with creation is that justice-righteousness is located prior to history, in the character of God, thence inscribed on the creation, and so expressed in the laws of Israel' (*God and Earthly Power*, 170–71).

3. The Individual and Social Justice

consequence; see, for instance, Prov. 10:5: 'A child who gathers in summer is prudent, but a child who sleeps in harvest brings shame'. Equally, parents are exhorted to action in order, it is hoped, to arrive at this happy consequence: 'Do not withhold discipline from your children; if you beat them with a rod, they will not die. If you beat them with the rod, you will save their lives from Sheol' (Prov. 23:13–14), and 13:24: 'Those who spare the rod hate their children, but those who love them are diligent to discipline them'. Equally, this same principle can be translated up into the divine realm, indicative of the fact that there is a principle at work here, not just some arbitrary rule: 'My child, do not despise the Lord's discipline or be weary of his reproof, for the Lord reproves the one he loves, as a father the son in whom he delights' (Prov. 3:11–12). Of course, while the principle holds good today that loving parents have to direct their children for their own good, and that children can avoid unhappy consequences by good behaviour, the means of application have changed, at least in many societies, for the simple reason that other observations have also come into play, such as that parents who are violent towards their children are not teaching them by example the way that they would want them to follow. But such modifications of the literal application of proverbs are wholly in line with their governing principle: act in accordance with the way that observation and experience show to be the most beneficial.

As a second example, we may move to Prov. 10:4, 'A slack hand causes poverty, but the hand of the diligent makes rich'. This is a prominent and recurring theme in Proverbs and one that, as a general rule, common sense could hardly deny. The consequences for behaviour are so obvious that they hardly need spelling out, but to cite just one familiar example, 'Go to the ant, you lazybones; consider its ways, and be wise. Without having any chief officer or ruler, it prepares its food in summer, and gathers its sustenance in harvest. How long will you lie there, O lazybones? When will you rise from your sleep? A little sleep, a little slumber, a little folding of the hands to rest, and poverty will come upon you like a robber, and want, like an armed warrior' (Prov. 6:6–11). The consequence of poverty resulting from laziness is thus explicitly a spur to action.

Of course, the writers are aware that there are exceptions to this general rule, and that is just as well, because we see still today, as they did then, that wealth and poverty are not awarded in direct proportion to effort put in. But in fact, that is not what the proverb says in the first place — it does not promise wealth in proportion to work but only that failure to work will lead to poverty. So this proverb deserves to be read in the context of the two that immediately precede it (and this we may do without getting bogged down in the debate about the extent to which the proverbs have been deliberately arranged in a specific sequence). First, 'Treasures gained by wickedness do not profit, but righteousness delivers from death' (10:2). So it is possible to gain wealth by illicit means (there is no comment on how much work is involved in that!), but the reader is urged to take a longer-term view of the situation: ultimately it will not endure, whereas righteousness will not necessarily make you rich but it will at least deliver from fatal consequences. Then comes the saying, 'The Lord does not let the righteous go hungry, but he thwarts the craving of the wicked' (10:3). Here again we note that the reward of the righteous is modest and that extravagant promises are avoided.

Now all this is not to say that success in life can be ascribed to the mechanical application of wisdom's rules and principles. However much the proverbs as a collection show more circumspection in what they say than some of their fiercer critics have allowed, the fact of course remains that there are exceptions even to these sayings, and other biblical books, not least Job and Ecclesiastes, tackle some of these in forceful and memorable ways. But in a sense we could say that there could not be a Job without Proverbs. It is only because Job's experience is such a blatant contradiction to standard observation that there is

3. The Individual and Social Justice

a problem to be discussed in the first place. And part, at least, of its answer is to move the source of the problem into the divine realm, where human observation no longer obtains. So there is an admitted limit on how far these kinds of proverb can take us in ultimate terms, but that does not mean that they should therefore be ignored as providing an important element, at least, in the basis on which decisions large and small should be taken in daily living.

As a third and final example we may take Prov. 10:19: 'When words are many, transgression is not lacking; but the prudent are restrained in speech'. On the understanding that in this verse 'transgression' refers to offence against other people rather than God, this verse probably means that in a human conflict situation endless prattling will only make matters worse, and that, as we might say today, 'least said, soonest mended'. There are times, therefore, when wisdom dictates the benefits of silence. This is not a blanket observation, therefore, but one that derives from and applies to a specific circumstance. The book of Proverbs in fact has a great deal to say about the wise use of speech and related matters, and application in each case is required in order to realize that the writers are not necessarily trying to generalize to the point of emptying their observations of any realism.

Examples such as these three could, of course, be multiplied. My point has been to illustrate two cardinal principles for our present concern. The first, which I have not documented in full here, is that for each of these examples numerous parallels could be drawn from other ancient Near Eastern sources; many examples are cited in the standard modern commentaries. These are therefore not what might popularly be called 'revealed truth' but they are the consequence of patient observation of how life works — in the social as much as in the natural realm, of course.

And secondly, it follows from this that the way to what the wise regard as a successful, and hence happy or blessed, life is to align oneself and one's conduct in accordance with those observations. This brings us back to the point that I sought to emphasize earlier, namely that in Israel (and here an element of distinctiveness does at last creep in) these principles were established in creation by wisdom, who was acting fully in accord with the divine plan in Proverbs 8. And in this, as we have seen, there is an unbroken continuity of principle from the work of the creator through to the establishment of royal rule and down through the scribal ranks to the common farmers and city-dwellers.

The link between theory and practice

It remains in this chapter finally to tie more closely together the first part of our discussion, where we undertook a brief survey of the use of language in Proverbs for social justice and the second part where we have tried to probe the basis on which this wisdom teaching is constructed.

In doing so, we may start by observing that poverty is spoken of in two somewhat different ways in Proverbs.[11] On the one hand, there are many proverbs which indicate that poverty may be the outcome especially of laziness, though it can also be said to be the outcome of other causes as well. Such sayings (and they are frequent) may legitimately be taken as warnings by the wealthy to others in their own circles or families against conduct that would lose them their privileged position. To that extent the somewhat cynical view may be justified that much language that initially sounds high-minded is actually self-serving, at least from a class-orientated point of view.

On the other hand, however, the converse point is not made, namely it is never said that poverty is always the immediate fault of the poor person, so that those scholars who have claimed that Proverbs is uniformly critical of the poor are mistaken. Folly, wickedness, excessive pleasure seeking and the like may reduce a wealthy person to poverty, but by no means

---

11 I am especially indebted to the analyses of Walter Houston in drawing these and the following conclusions: *Contending for Justice*, 117–26, and 'The Role of the Poor in Proverbs'.

are all the poor in that situation for those reasons alone; some just are members of the poorer classes. In some cases they may themselves have suffered injustice: 'The field of the poor may yield much food, but it is swept away through injustice' (Prov. 13:23), but even here it should be noted first that the subject of the saying seems to have been classed as 'poor' even before suffering injustice, and second the degree of poverty that allows him to be classified as 'poor' may not be as great as we might at first suppose, since he at least has a field that he may cultivate. Elsewhere, furthermore, there are proverbs which speak of the poor with a degree of compassion, and at no point is there any implication that the poor deserve their position because they have all been lazy or the like. Thus we should recognize that although poverty may serve as a warning to the wealthy, that is not the whole sum of the story about poverty in Proverbs. Some people just are poor, and it is then of interest to see what would be the appropriate response to that by others.

First, we find a number of sayings which simply encourage a kind or generous attitude: 'Those who despise their neighbours are sinners, but happy are those who are kind to the poor' (Prov. 14:21), or 'Those who are generous are blessed, for they share their bread with the poor' (Prov. 22:9). This, however, is not merely self-sacrificial, because there are other sayings, quite unexpected, which may be laid alongside these to indicate that even such kindness is not ultimately costly: 'Some give freely, yet grow all the richer; others withhold what is due, and only suffer want. A generous person will be enriched, and one who gives water will get water' (Prov. 11:24–25); 'Whoever gives to the poor will lack nothing, but one who turns a blind eye will get many a curse' (Prov. 28:27).

Second, this apparent paradox may be partially explained, at least, by those sayings that put a more overtly theological slant on this by relating care for the poor with the attitude of the creator God. 'Those who oppress the poor insult their Maker, but those who are kind to the needy honour him' (Prov. 14:31; cf. 17:5); 'The Lord tears down the house of the proud, but maintains the widow's boundaries' (Prov. 15:25); 'The rich and the poor have this in common: the Lord is the maker of them all' (Prov. 22:2; cf. 29:13); and 'Do not rob the poor because they are poor, or crush the afflicted at the gate; for the Lord pleads their cause and despoils the life of those who despoil them' (Prov. 22:22–23).

These sayings too, however, may be balanced by a couple which indicate that even in this case the Lord ensures that the generous do not lose out: 'Whoever is kind to the poor lends to the Lord, and will be repaid in full' (Prov. 19:17), and 'Honour the Lord with your substance and with the first fruits of all your produce; then your barns will be filled with plenty, and your vats will be bursting with wine' (Prov. 3:9–10). There is thus a balance between what happens at the purely human level, as in our first group of sayings, and in imitation of the divine, as in the second.

Putting these sayings together suggests that underlying a concern for the poor in Proverbs are the views that (i) poverty is sometimes just one of those things, a part of the created order which there is no need to question in ultimate terms, that (ii) the proper response is, where possible, to imitate the creator who made things that way but who shows impartial care for rich and poor alike, so that (iii) generosity is natural and not itself impoverishing, since it fits with the created order that we find in God's world.

This may seem an initially strange way of viewing things, but I suggest that at base it is trying to urge social justice as the best form of natural order for the good of society, including its ruling classes. It is not distinctive to Israel in general terms, though its tie to the creator certainly invites interpretation in a uniquely 'Israelite' way. But most importantly, it is not urged by way of command or rebuke but is rather encouraged by a process of observation which makes it seem natural and good so

3. The Individual and Social Justice

that people will wish to adopt that approach for reasons of good sense along with personal and social well-being. Any element of 'revelation' that is necessary to stimulate this is well within the bounds of natural observation. Though it can be expressed in 'prophetic' terms in the prologue, that is not its source so far as the book goes in its present form.

4
Prophetic Justice

Thus far we have looked at a number of ways in which the Old Testament's concern for social justice seems to derive less from any specifically Israelite religious or other such specific concern and rather to be the product of inspired reflection within the context of the wider world in which Israel lived. Furthermore, I have suggested, on the basis of the evidence of the book of Proverbs, that the understanding of, and motivation for, the practice of social justice was, for most purposes, derived from reflection on the way the world has been created and how, in the long run, one may best fit in with it so far as the treatment of others, and particularly the poor, is concerned.

In this chapter I want to turn to the prophets, and especially the earliest of the written prophets, in order to test the extent to which the situation here is the same or radically different. It is likely that most reasonably well informed Bible readers would expect the difference here to be quite marked. These are the books to which appeal is most frequently made when preachers or others want to draw attention to what may be presented as distinctively biblical; indeed, the adjective 'prophetic' is popular in just such contexts. I shall try to show that this is justified to some extent, but not to the extent that many people suppose.

4. Prophetic Justice

Furthermore, when we turn to ask of this on what one's sense of justice should be based we shall find a solution that is far from that which might be popularly expected.[1]

As in the last chapter, so here I shall begin with a survey of some of the prominent passages where the word pair 'justice and righteousness' occurs. As with Proverbs, so in the prophets this does not by any means exhaust the writers' attention to our theme, but it is again better to proceed from the more to the less certain in order not to get sidetracked unwittingly from what is most central to our study.

Isaiah

It may be easiest to begin with the writings of Isaiah of Jerusalem, an eighth-century Judean prophet whose preserved sayings are included within parts of Isaiah 1–39. While the critical issues regarding how much of these chapters may legitimately be ascribed to Isaiah himself are very controversial, most middle-of-the-road scholars would agree that we have more material from him than from any other of his near contemporaries. Furthermore, this is a subject that I have treated at greater length elsewhere[2] and so can summarize my principal conclusions here in a way that should make for greatest clarity as a firm starting point.

Our two words occur together some dozen times in these chapters, and from these we can immediately see that they cover almost as wide a range of concerns as we saw in Proverbs and that they are regarded as fundamental to Isaiah's portrayal of the ideal society.

---

1 For a recent scholarly analysis of this question with whose main conclusions I find myself in broad agreement though he draws a sharper distinction between Amos and Isaiah on the one hand and Hosea and Jeremiah on the other, see Francolino J. Gonçalves, 'Fondements du message social des prophètes', in A. Lemaire (ed.), *Congress Volume Ljubljana 2007* (Supplements to *Vetus Testamentum* 133; Leiden: Brill, 2010), 597–620.

2 Williamson, *Variations on a Theme*, 18–29.

In chapter 1, for example, they are used to highlight what is regarded as a past golden age, presumably the days of David and Solomon,[3] when Jerusalem 'was full of justice, righteousness lodged in her' (v. 21). The loss of those virtues is reflected now in a variety of ills, including murder, perversion of the legal system by bribery and other such forms of corruption, and the failure to attend to the legal right of the orphan and widow. In my opinion, some of these elements are likely to have been added to the list by later redactors, for reasons which need not detain us here.[4] It is probable that concern about the perversion of the legal system was the earliest element, and thus it is of interest to see how (based no doubt on Isa. 1:17) this is amplified and illustrated by the stereotypical reference to the orphan and widow. As we have seen previously, this is standard in the ancient Near East, so that in all probability the editor is in effect equating Isaiah's concerns with a recognized way of saying that 'everything has gone to the dogs'.

The word pair occurs also in a prominent position at the end of the song of the vineyard in chapter 5. Here, the singer reveals himself to be God, who gives expression to his anguish at the way in which all the privileges and blessings that he had bestowed on his people have been spurned in a way that leads away from social justice to unbridled violence: 'He expected justice, but saw bloodshed; righteousness, but heard a cry!' (Isa. 5:7b). In noting the nature of these negative qualities, we should be aware of the

---

3   We may note that in 2 Sam. 8:15 the members of David's 'cabinet' are introduced with the claim that 'David administered "justice and righteousness" to all his people', while the Queen of Sheba declares as the climax of her encomium that God has made Solomon king 'to execute "justice and righteousness"' (1 Kgs 10:9). They are thus both depicted as an example of the ideal ruler according to the psalmists (e.g. Ps. 45:6–7; 72:1) and prophets.

4   I have set the reasons out in full in my commentary, *A Critical and Exegetical Commentary on Isaiah 1–27*, 1: *Commentary on Isaiah 1–5* (Internatioanl Critical Ccommentary; London: T & T Clark, 2006), 120–46.

4. Prophetic Justice

fact that the choice of vocabulary here is determined by word-play in the Hebrew, 'bloodshed' and 'a cry' echoing the words for 'justice' and 'righteousness'. But even if we make allowance for that, it is clear that the two sides of illegitimate violence are here highlighted, the one, bloodshed, being the same in effect as what Isaiah portrayed in 1:15 as the climax of social sin which completely negates the effectiveness of religious practice and the other being the cry of distress by the oppressed.

Despite what some commentators have written, there is no apparent requirement to interpret this verse as referring to the oppression of the poor by the rich or the like. Violence and its converse in the cry of despair are not in any way limited to cross-class practice but are found within classes as often as not, and equally they can apply to the lower acting against the higher just as much as the reverse. This may therefore be taken quite simply as a characterization of the evils of society generally as Isaiah observed them.

A third example which most scholars would ascribe to Isaiah comes at 28:16–17:

> Therefore thus says the Lord God,
> See, I am laying in Zion a foundation stone,
>   a tested stone,
> a precious cornerstone, a sure foundation:
>   'One who trusts will not panic.'
> And I will make justice the line,
>   and righteousness the plummet:
> hail will sweep away the refuge of lies,
>   and waters will overwhelm the shelter.

Amidst several uncertainties regarding the interpretation of these two verses, one thing seems clear, namely that social justice will be at the very foundation of the society or community that God plans to rebuild in Zion. This was the name of Jerusalem used to depict the ideal society of earlier days in Isa. 1:21 that we looked at previously. As we saw, it was the corruption of those elements that heralded Zion's degeneration from faithful city to 'whore', and here we learn that it will be their restoration that will mark her regeneration.

From the three cardinal passages noted so far, then, we can see without difficulty that social justice is fundamental to Isaiah's vision for the ideal society. It was practised in the glorious past and will be fully restored again in the future, whereas its corruption in the present is the cause for punitive judgment that he anticipates in the shorter-term future. As far as we have seen so far, it is more closely tied to the judicial system in Isaiah than in Proverbs, though in Isa. 1:21–23 it had a wider application than the processes of the law courts alone, and this is also the implication of Isa. 5:7.

Furthermore, while Isa. 5:7 itself has no necessary class implications it is interesting to note that an interpretation of this passage occurs in Isa. 3:13–15 where such an element is introduced:

> The Lord rises to argue his case;
>   he stands to judge the peoples.
> [14] The Lord enters into judgement
>   with the elders and princes of his people:
> It is you who have devoured the vineyard;
>   the spoil of the poor is in your houses.
> [15] What do you mean by crushing my people,
>   by grinding the face of the poor? says the Lord God of hosts.

The link with 5:1–7 is clearly made by the line 'it is you who have devoured the vineyard', and in addition there is a further link by the use of the rare word for destroy/devour in this line and in 5:5. In 3:13–15, however, it is clear that the prime example of lack of social justice is seen precisely in the oppression of the poor by the rich with its talk of 'the spoil of the poor' being in the houses of the elders and princes (v. 14) and with the language in v. 15 of 'grinding the face of the poor'. This looks like an application of the more general song of the vineyard in

4. Prophetic Justice

a more specific manner, just as we saw was also attempted by the addition of the orphan and widow in Isa. 1:23. A possible explanation of what is going on here will be offered a little later.

In Proverbs we saw that the language of social justice was closely aligned with concerns to fit one's life in with the created order. In Isaiah, by contrast, these concerns have a much more royal basis: these are the values which it is the responsibility of the king to institute and uphold as the basis of his rule, and from that, in a descending social hierarchy, others should imitate him in their mutual social dealings. This royal perspective is apparent in two well-known passages.

First, in a verse which I have argued should be regarded as proverbial, we read: 'Behold, a king should reign in the interests of righteousness, and princes rule for the furtherance of justice' (Isa. 32:1, my translation). Here we see clearly that, whether or not he is citing a familiar proverb, Isaiah views social justice as a primary responsibility of the king and his closest associates. This is also, in fact, a common notion in the book of Proverbs. We saw something of this in the previous chapter, and here it is worth pointing out how closely our verse in Isaiah compares with Prov. 8:15–16 which I cited there: wisdom, it may be recalled, asserts that 'by me kings reign, and rulers decree what is just; by me rulers rule, and nobles, all who govern rightly', and the overlap of Hebrew vocabulary between these passages is striking. Many other proverbs, however, assert much the same thing.[5]

One or two of these verses link the royal execution of social justice with the establishment of the royal throne, for instance 'if a king judges the poor with equity, his throne will be established for ever' (Prov. 29:14). This too finds something of a parallel in Isaiah where, in the second well-known passage that I cite in this regard, Isa. 9:7, it is said of the royal child of the Davidic family that he will 'establish [same verb] and uphold' his throne 'with justice and with righteousness'.

---

5 See, for instance, Prov. 16:10, 13; 20:8, 26; 29:4, 14; 31:4–5.

There can thus be no doubt that there are a number of similarities between Isaiah and Proverbs in this regard, and of course there have been some scholars who have argued on this basis that Isaiah must have belonged to the same class of 'the wise' (royal scribes?) as the authors of Proverbs. This seems to me to be an unnecessary (though not impossible) conclusion to draw. Rather, given that both he and they came from Jerusalem in possibly a not too separated chronological horizon, it is preferable to see them sharing some basic cultural and ideological values.[6]

Within these similarities, however, it is interesting also to note the particularities which make each distinct. So far as Isaiah is concerned, this relates, in my view, to how he presents the source of his understanding. For the wisdom writers, as we saw, it concerned their understanding of how the Creator established the principles on which the world works as wisdom, so that their responsibility was to probe that wisdom and to align their lives with it. For Isaiah, by contrast, his understanding seems to have been based most particularly on his vision of the Lord as king, enthroned and exalted, as depicted most strikingly in Isaiah 6. To cut a long story short, Isaiah's view of the world was thus strongly hierarchical: God as king was supreme; under him was his human king in Zion; and lower down there were in turn the various royal officials who should each take the ideal patterns of their rule and way of life from those above them. Only as each did this effectively in ultimate imitation of the divine king, whose ways were supremely just and righteous, would society be administered in an ideal manner. Conversely, as they subverted those values and standards in one way or another, so negative judgment would be the result for them and for their nation.

---

6   Hugh G.M. Williamson, 'Isaiah and the Wise', in John Day, Robert P. Gordon and Hugh G.M. Williamson (eds.), *Wisdom in Ancient Israel: Studies in Honour of J.A. Emerton* (Cambridge: Cambridge University Press, 1995), 133-41.

4. Prophetic Justice

Almost inevitably, the human understanding of the divine, not least when projected as a form of kingship, reflects something of our knowledge of the human counterpart.[7] This is obviously the case with regard to the language used, but in fact it is difficult not to suppose that it does not also include a projection of what might be regarded as the ideal of that to which the human institution aspires. In other words, when we speak of God as king (or, indeed, as father, shepherd, or whatever else), we mostly conjure up an image of the best of each category and envisage God as fulfilling that in some perfect manner.

If that is approximately also the case with Isaiah (and this does not in the least threaten any doctrine of inspiration, of course), then we may assume that what he wanted to convey by saying that 'in the year that king Uzziah died I saw the Lord sitting on a throne, high and lofty' (Isa. 6:1) was that God met the highest and loftiest ideal of kingship that he was able to conceive. In Proverbs, the human throne could be established on righteousness. In Isaiah, the human throne would be established as it imitated the divine throne, and this could only be given content not by probing wisdom but rather by idealizing the notions of human kingship that were current. And, as we saw in a previous chapter, that included concerns for social justice in no small measure, as I sought to show by my selective survey of the stated ideals of kingship from outside Israel.

In line with this conclusion, we should also recall that so far as Isaiah of Jerusalem is concerned, there is no indication anywhere that what we consider as the fundamental tenets of justice as enshrined in the stipulations of the Sinai covenant were in any way normative for him directly. At any rate, I do not know of any reference to such material in authentically Isaianic sayings. They just do not seem to be the source of his ethical and social principles.

---

7   This is helpfully explored by Marc Z. Brettler, *God is King: Understanding an Israelite Metaphor* (*Journal for the Study of the Old Testament*, Supplement Series 76; Sheffield: Sheffield Academic Press, 1989).

I conclude, therefore, that important as concerns for social justice most certainly were to Isaiah, he derived his understanding of them from the royal traditions of Zion, understood in his theology as being in turn derivative from the divine king. Access to such knowledge therefore came about through knowledge of the royal traditions and ideals of Judah and her ancient neighbours. They are certainly 'theologized' (if I may coin such a term), but their source is rational reflection rather than divine imposition.

And this, I suggest, explains the elements of interpretation of social justice in class terms that we noted earlier. It is not that the references to the orphan and widow in Isa. 1:23 or to the poor whose faces are ground down by oppression in Isa. 3:15 derive from some isolated sense of 'prophetic' inspiration. Rather, they are the rational application of the principles of a hierarchically ordered society in which those in positions of privileged responsibility are not wicked *de facto*. As was ideally acknowledged in countries other than Judah as well (though probably enacted as infrequently in the one as in the other), the role of such people included the social and legal care of those who were not in a position to undertake that for themselves. Social justice is an acknowledged responsibility downwards, so to speak, and Isaiah was doing no more than giving forceful expression to a widely acknowledged ideal. His words do not become more powerful by being elevated into some isolated category; in fact, they would become less challenging because they would seem to become unattainable. By giving expression to that which was already in every heart, as it were, he in fact made the challenge and the condemnation even more telling.

Amos

While this hardly does justice to the wealth of relevant material in the first part of the book of Isaiah it must suffice for now as indicative of the fact that his teaching in this realm, though

4. Prophetic Justice

passionate and challenging now as then, is not so original as the popular label 'prophetic' often implies. While there will be more to be said of him further on, perhaps we should do better, then, next to consider his slightly earlier predecessor Amos, a man of Judean origin, like Isaiah, but one whose words were addressed primarily to the northern kingdom of Israel, a kingdom where, so general consensus has it, the sinaitic law (in whatever shape or form) was more authoritative than in Judah.

Our thematic word pair occurs three times in Amos, all in the central group of sayings (chapters 3–6) which are generally regarded as part of the basic core of the book.

Two of the passages are somewhat similar: 'Ah, you that turn justice to wormwood, and bring righteousness to the ground' (Amos 5:7), and 'you have turned justice into poison and the fruit of righteousness into wormwood' (Amos 6:12). The first of these follows on an exhortation to 'seek the Lord and live' (Amos 5:6), though the implications of that are uncertain. Normally we should expect it to include, at the least, some form of cultic service, but in the immediately preceding passage the same words are apparently used in sharp contrast with formal religion: 'seek me and live; but do not seek Bethel, and do not enter into Gilgal or cross over to Beersheba', these apparently being significant cultic sites in that period. A wedge seems to be being driven between formal religion and the true seeking of God through the practice of social justice.

This is reinforced by some passages just a little later in the chapter where the same contrast is drawn even more clearly: 'seek good and not evil, that you may live. ... Hate evil and love good, and establish justice in the gate' (Amos 5:14–15). Together with other material in the surrounding context (see especially 5:10–12) it seems clear that Amos is elevating equitable justice in the local courts above religious observance. And this ties in closely with the most famous of all his sayings in this regard, which is the third where our word pair appears, towards the end of this same chapter:

> I hate, I despise your festivals,
>> and I take no delight in your solemn assemblies.
> Even though you offer me your burnt-offerings and grain-offerings,
>> I will not accept them;
> And the offerings of well-being of your fatted animals
>> I will not look upon.
> Take away from me the noise of your songs;
>> I will not listen to the melody of your harps.
> But let justice roll down like waters,
>> and righteousness like an ever-flowing stream.
>
> (Amos 5:21–24)

No matter how much we seek to moderate the rhetoric here by speaking of strong affirmation of the positive by denial of the negative, the conclusion cannot be avoided that at the very least Amos here sets social justice ahead of formal religious observance, in line with what we have already seen previously in the passage.

So far as the present full text of the Bible is concerned, this conclusion is already striking, given that the Mosaic law is by no means deficient in its regulation of all aspects of the formal Israelite cult. It is true that much of that material comes in the priestly portions of the Pentateuch which most scholars (I am sure correctly) maintain was not yet codified by the time of Amos. But even if we accept that literary-critical conclusion, it does not mean that there were not some earlier cultic codes which almost certainly were known by Amos and his contemporaries, and even were we to deny that the principle would still remain that the cult, with its psalms, offerings and festivals, was at the very heart of Israel's communal religious remembrance of God's past and gracious dealings with his people. It is therefore difficult to suppose that Amos simultaneously looked to the same source for his inspiration with regard to social justice.

An alternative approach is suggested by the context in which the saying in Amos 6:12 is set. It follows immediately

4. Prophetic Justice

upon the following questions: 'Do horses run on rocks? Does one plough the sea[8] with oxen?' The answer is, of course, no, it would be absurd and nobody would be so stupid as to try. It is equally absurd, Amos then goes on to say, to turn justice into poison and the fruit of righteousness into wormwood. In other words, religious law is not necessary to dictate the requirement that justice and righteousness should be practised; it is obvious to any right-thinking person who takes God seriously. This seems to be a very 'wisdom-like' conclusion to arrive at, not directly in the sense that Amos would have formulated his thinking in the same terms as Proverbs but in that both ultimately depend on favouring social justice as something that is self-evidently right. Strange as it may seem, in other words, we find the most strident prophetic invective to be based on natural justice as much as the wisdom writers were.

Hosea and Micah

Before extending our discussion of the eighth century prophets wider than passages in which the word pair occurs, I should add briefly for the sake of completeness that it occurs once each in Hosea and Micah. At Hos. 2:19 (Hebrew, 2:21) we find it as part of the expression of God's character as he moves to restore his wayward people under the guise of a man 'betrothing' a girl to himself: 'I will take you for my

---

8   This represents a small and widely agreed emendation to the Hebrew text, namely the division into two of what is now one Hebrew word. Without the emendation the line reads: 'Does one plough with oxen?', to which the answer is obviously 'yes', so making the saying ineffective in context. If the emendation is not favoured, it becomes necessary to understand the line as meaning 'does one plough there [i.e. on rocks] with oxen?', but it is difficult to know whether this can be justified. For a full discussion of the various possibilities, see Shalom M. Paul, *Amos: A Commentary on the Book of Amos* (Minneapolis, MN: Fortress, 1991), 218–19. The issue does not affect the substance of my argument above.

wife in righteousness and in justice, in steadfast love, and in mercy'. Just as we saw that in Isaiah there was an element of human imitation of the divine royal character in this regard, so here we have a similar pattern but this time in more intimate human terms, and interestingly it is further qualified by words of compassion and grace — an indication that those who would be imitators of God should have that 'bias' built into their exercise of social justice. A better understanding of God's character, in other words, could have had a restricting influence on the kind of abuses in the local courts that so exercised Amos.

A similar emphasis is apparent in Mic. 7:9, even though this is part of a passage which was almost certainly written considerably later than the eighth century. Here, the author speaks of the inevitability of his suffering God's rebuke because of his sin, but a brighter future also awaits: 'until he takes my side and executes judgment for me. He will bring me out to the light; I shall see his vindication (literally, his righteousness for me)'. As in Hosea, therefore, we see these characteristics which we normally consider in human terms prefigured by God in a manner which speaks of benefit for the afflicted.

To sum up this survey of the use of 'justice and righteousness' in the writings of the eighth century prophets, we may say that there is certainly an emphasis on the more strictly legal aspect of its usage but that this does not exhaust its significance. In addition, there are clear indications that the exhortation to practise righteousness and justice was encouraged with respect to those lower down the socio-economic pile than oneself, but that there was included in this a sufficient flexibility as to who was where on the scale to indicate that this was more than just a tirade against the rich on behalf of the poor. Rather, it derived from an understanding of society that was hierarchical in structure and in which, in imitation of God himself, the enjoyment of privilege was regarded as including

4. Prophetic Justice

a responsibility for those less privileged. At no point, so far as I can see, is this structure itself critiqued; it is taken as a given and appropriate behaviour within it is expected.

A wider survey of Amos

We should now extend our survey to look at some of the relevant material that is not specifically highlighted by our two key terms (though sometimes one or the other may appear on its own). How far has what we have seen so far been typical and characteristic, and how far should we modify our initial picture?

Certainly in Amos (to start with the earliest of the prophets) we have already seen that there are indications that social justice is especially focused on the need to ensure equity in the local courts with a bias towards ensuring that those lower down the social order are not disadvantaged. This same principle is widened to apply also to spheres that lie outside the formalities of the law and the courts.

We may take the opening verses of Amos 4 as a powerful example:

> Hear this word, you cows of Bashan
>   who are on Mount Samaria,
> who oppress the poor, who crush the needy,
>   who say to their husbands, 'Bring something to drink!'
> The Lord God has sworn by his holiness:
>   The time is surely coming upon you,
> when they shall take you away with hooks,
>   even the last of you with fish-hooks.
> Through breaches in the wall you shall leave,
>   each one straight ahead;
>   and you shall be flung out into Harmon, says the Lord.

This address to the women of Samaria in Amos 4:1–3 castigates them for oppressing the poor and crushing the needy, though quite how they do so is not spelt out. In my opinion we should take two clues from the context to help us understand this condemnation better. Fist and most obviously, they demand of their husbands, 'bring something to drink'. Second, more indirectly, by calling them 'cows of Bashan' Amos was not just being rude but was framing his invective more pointedly. Bashan is the high plateau to the east of the Sea of Galilee, which includes what we know of as the Golan Heights, and it was famed in antiquity for its great fertility due both to the quality of its soil and its more plentiful rainfall than most of the surrounding regions.[9] Elsewhere it is singled out, therefore, for the excellence of its agriculture and pasturage (Mic. 7:14) and for its fine oaks (Isa. 2:13; Ezek. 27:6; Zech. 11:2) as well as its domestic animals (Deut. 32:14; Ezek. 39:18; Ps. 22:12). When Amos refers to the cows of Bashan, therefore, it is likely that he has in mind their well-fed nature which would be evident just by looking at them. There is thus a probable reference in this passage to the unnecessarily indulgent lifestyles of these women with regard to both food and drink. Now it seems unlikely that they would have directly and consciously oppressed and crushed the poor. Rather, I suspect that the reference to their demands of their husbands is to indicate that their oppression was at second hand, so to speak; in order to keep up with their requirements, the husbands were having to take short cuts in their dealings with others.

Incidentally, the people referred to as being oppressed need not be just small independent farmers, as is often assumed. It could equally be employees of the husbands on their own farms or estates, those who produced goods of various kinds and the merchants or middlemen who acted on the husbands' behalf. In fact, in a recent study Houston has demonstrated how frequently the references to oppression refer to town or city

---

9 See Denis Baly, *The Geography of the Bible* (new and revised edn; Guildford: Lutterworth, 1974), 213–16; William S. LaSor, 'Bashan', in Geoffrey W. Bromiley (ed.), *The International Standard Bible Encyclopedia* (Grand Rapids, Michigan: Eerdmans, 1979), 1:436–37.

4. Prophetic Justice

dwellers rather than to the agricultural communities that mostly lived in the villages, where, he claims, archaeological evidence is not indicative of extreme poverty.[10]

This conclusion is exegetically and historically important. For too long scholars have simply assumed that the crisis of oppression to which the prophets refer related almost exclusively to small farmers, and the explanation given was based on more recent, western capitalist models of mortgages and foreclosures. Although this may have happened from time to time, it is clear that the notion of a crisis which can be wheeled out to explain texts over a range of several hundred years (i.e. from at least the eighth century BCE in the prophets to the fifth century BCE, as testified in Nehemiah 5) stretches credulity. Recent research has begun to take far more seriously the nature of agricultural practices as employed then as well as more recently in some other, though not wholly dissimilar, societies. The role of patronage, for instance, is quite different from anything with which most of us are closely familiar, so that it would be a mistake to try to press ancient Israel into a more modern western mode.[11] But that does not empty the prophetic rhetoric of its force; it merely sends us back to the texts to investigate more carefully what class of people and what sort of labour are being referred to.

---

10 Walter J. Houston, 'Exit the Oppressed Peasant? Rethinking the Background of Social Criticism in the Prophets', in John Day (ed.), *Prophecy and Prophets in Ancient Israel: Proceedings of the Oxford Old Testament Seminar* (Library of Hebrew Bible/Old Testament Studies 531; New York: T & T Clark, 2010), 101–16. His research in this area was stimulated in particular by a series of articles by, as well as personal communication with, the Israeli archaeologist Avraham Faust. These have now been worked into a book, which at present is available only in modern Hebrew: *Israelite Society in the Period of the Monarchy: An Archaeological Examination* (Jerusalem: Yad Izhak Ben-Zvi, 2005); an English version, entitled *The Archaeology of Israelite Society in Iron Age II* should soon become available, published by Eisenbrauns, Winona Lake.
11 For a somewhat extreme presentation of this relatively new approach, see Philippe Guillaume, *Land, Credit and Crisis: Agrarian Finance in the Hebrew Bible* (London: Equinox, 2011).

Although this is not my main point here, it is difficult not to draw an analogy with the observation that many of our western demands for cheap goods of all kinds often cause others in manufacturing or trade to oppress their workers on our behalf. We may be as ignorant of this as the women of Samaria were, but in Amos's view this would not excuse us. We should take some trouble to inform ourselves about whether the goods and services we buy are oppressive, both in terms of those who provide them and those who transport them and where possible we should surely move to the use of fairtrade items. This is a big subject which I cannot open up here in full, but the starting point must be the need to educate ourselves better as to the consequences of our consumer society. As with Amos, we should know better than we do.

The unnecessary luxury of which this passage speaks is expressed more than once elsewhere in Amos as well. The opening verses of chapter 6 are as clear an example as any:

> Alas for those who are at ease in Zion,
>   and for those who feel secure on Mount Samaria,
> the notables of the first of the nations,
>   to whom the house of Israel resorts!
> ² Cross over to Calneh, and see;
>   from there go to Hamath the great;
> then go down to Gath of the Philistines.
> Are you better than these kingdoms?
>   Or is your territory greater than their territory,
> ³ O you that put far away the evil day,
>   and bring near a reign of violence?
>
> ⁴ Alas for those who lie on beds of ivory,
>   and lounge on their couches,
> and eat lambs from the flock,
>   and calves from the stall;
> ⁵ who sing idle songs to the sound of the harp,
>   and like David improvise on instruments of music;

4. Prophetic Justice

> ⁶ who drink wine from bowls,
>   and anoint themselves with the finest oils,
>   but are not grieved over the ruin of Joseph!
> ⁷ Therefore they shall now be the first to go into exile,
>   and the revelry of the loungers shall pass away.
>
> (Amos 6:1–7)

On what basis, however, does Amos come to condemn such behaviour? Does he quote some biblical law that the people should have known and which they were disobeying? Apparently not. In fact, in chapter 6, although verse 2 is almost certainly a later addition to the passage,[12] it draws attention to the fate of several foreign cities, so that rather as in the oracles against the nations in chapters 1–2, we have to assume that the basis for judgment is wider than Israelite law alone.

In addition, however, there is an important but frequently overlooked key to the whole passage in v. 7, where there is one of the very few references in the Old Testament to a type of religio-social banqueting institution known as a *marzeach*. This is the Hebrew word which occurs in v. 7 where in the NRSV it is translated 'revelry': 'Therefore they shall now be the first to go into exile, and the revelry of the loungers shall pass away'.

This type of banquet is known from other North-West Semitic sources as well, and it is also mentioned directly at Jer. 16:5. There may be allusions to it elsewhere even if the word itself does not occur, though of course the extent to which that is the case is disputed.[13] One possibility is that it may also lie behind the allusions

---

12 The verse faces all sorts of difficulties of interpretation, which only add to the problem of deciding about its literary origin. There is a recent helpful survey of all these topics in Tchavdar S. Hadjiev, *The Composition and Redaction of the Book of Amos* (Beihefte zur Zeitschrift für die alttestamentliche Wissenschaft 393; Berlin: de Gruyter, 2009), 170–73.

13 The whole subject is fully, clearly and sensibly discussed in John L. McLaughlin, *The marzeah in the Prophetic Literature: References and Allusions in Light of the Extra-Biblical Evidence* (Supplements to *Vetus Testamentum* 86; Leiden: Brill, 2001).

to eating and drinking that we looked at in Amos 4. As is known from elsewhere, this institutional banqueting was characterized by heavy drinking and elaborate feasting, as mentioned here at Amos 6:4–6, so that almost inevitably it was the preserve of the wealthiest classes alone. It is not directly mentioned in the mosaic law at all. Amos's objection to it is clear in 6:6, and it ties in closely with what we have already seen in the previous chapters of his book. He does not condemn the institution as such, as though it somehow contravened established Israelite religious practice, but rather he objects to the attitude that it displayed of personal indulgence with no regard for the wider social division which it pointed up: after listing many of the banquet's excesses, he laments 'but they are not grieved over the ruin of Joseph'. In other words it is another example, as at the end of chapter 5, where he objects to religious practice as offensive if it disregards issues of social justice. A religion that is divisive is self-condemned, and the punishment is again not so much one of the covenantal curses as a straightforward case of reversal of status: of the 'first' in society it is said 'therefore they shall now be the first to go into exile' (Amos 6:7).

I conclude, therefore, that some of the most familiar passages in Amos relating to social justice in the wider sense than just the legal in fact demonstrate a similar basis and rationale to those we examined in the first place. The level of the rhetoric may have been stepped up, but the underlying theology is the same. Such behaviour is self-evidently offensive and that should have been as obvious to Israel as Amos clearly thought it should have been to her neighbours whom his book condemns in its introductory oracles.

A wider survey of Isaiah

Turning to the first part of the book of Isaiah in search of wider examples than those already discussed, we find that there is, of course, a wealth of material that cannot all be discussed here.

4. Prophetic Justice

Two observations suggest that we need not worry that we shall be short changed by having only a brief discussion, however.

First, among all the invective in these chapters we find that much lies outside the strict sphere of social justice. Most of the woe sayings in 5:8–24, for instance, are directed against other forms of evil which may, it is true, involve social abuse, but that is not explicitly spelt out. We may therefore conclude that this was not Isaiah's main concern in these instances. For instance, the first saying, in vv. 8–10, deals with those who 'join house to house, who add field to field'. This is often explained with reference to oppressive lending and debt systems, but of course that is speculative, and in any case, the agricultural system as a whole functioned for the large part on the basis of short-term loans and the like, so that even though sometimes individuals may have got into difficulties as a result, it is not easy to affirm that the system as such was corrupt. In the current saying, by contrast, the major element of the invective is directed against unbridled avarice, not the manipulation of capital advantage, so that it would be a mistake to lump such a saying in with others as though it had no distinctive voice of its own.

Second, where we find sayings that have social justice as a particular element, they do not necessarily add anything that is new to the points we have already discussed. In the series of woes in ch. 5, for instance, there is only one that comes into this category, namely vv. 22–23, where we find:

> Ah, you who are heroes in drinking wine
>   and valiant at mixing drink,
> who acquit the guilty for a bribe,
>   and deprive the innocent of their rights!

The second two lines are quite similar to what we found already in Isa. 1:21–26 and in the book of Proverbs. Interestingly that commonplace is here juxtaposed with condemnation of excessive drinking, a subject also broached independently earlier in v. 11. Now, there is nothing in the law as such about drinking too much, so that any such condemnation must be based on a commonly agreed standard of reasonable behaviour; in other words, it fits exactly with the pattern of thinking that we have detected elsewhere. More than that, however, the collocation with erring in justice is also paralleled in a number of passages, of which interestingly we may put at the top of the list Prov. 31:4–5 (and vv. 6–9 following make a similar point):

> It is not for kings to drink wine,
> > or for rulers to desire strong drink;
> > or else they will drink and forget what has been decreed,
> > and will pervert the rights of all the afflicted.

There are similar concerns expressed also at Amos 2:8, where the prophet seems to criticize those who use unjustly gained fines to buy wine and strong drink, and also, though less pointedly, in the passages in Amos 4:1 and 6:6 that we introduced previously. Finally, elsewhere in Isaiah the same connection is made, for at 28:7 those who 'reel with wine and stagger with strong drink' are also those who 'stumble in giving judgment'.

All this, I suggest, merely serves to reinforce the conclusion that even such fundamental issues as the abuse of the legal system by the wealthy at the expense of the poor was regarded as self-evidently wrong and anti-social, just like heavy drinking, which could, of course, sometimes be part of the cause. There is no need of a law to tell us it is wrong.

If much of Isaiah's material thus fits neatly into the pattern of what we have already seen, there is one passage which perhaps takes us a step further, namely Isa. 10:1–4:

> Ah, you who make iniquitous decrees,
> > who write oppressive statutes,
> to turn aside the needy from justice
> > and to rob the poor of my people of their right,
> that widows may be your spoil,
> > and that you may make the orphans your prey!

4. Prophetic Justice

> What will you do on the day of punishment,
> > in the calamity that will come from far away?
> To whom will you flee for help,
> > and where will you leave your wealth,
> so as not to crouch among the prisoners
> > or fall among the slain?
> For all this, his anger has not turned away;
> > his hand is stretched out still.

This paragraph has provoked a good deal of discussion among the commentators. It starts with 'Woe!' (NRSV 'Ah'), which seems to link it with the series of woe-sayings in chapter 5. It finishes, however, with a pair of lines about God's ongoing anger, and these are like a refrain that is found also at 9:12, 17 and 21 (see also 5:25). The passage thus seems to link by its beginning or its ending with two previous separate series of passages. As may be imagined, this has led to all sorts of suggestions for rearranging the passages so as to make them fit together more tidily, but in my opinion, apart from the completely hypothetical nature of any such proposal, it is probably mistaken in this case. Although the case cannot be argued here in detail, the easiest suggestion is to see this passage as a deliberately framed piece to round off the two previous series. It will not have been an original member of either, but was added at some stage in the book's compilation in order to bring a major section of the book to a close.

If that is correct, it follows that the indictment may not be from Isaiah himself but from one of the book's later editors. As a consequence, we may conclude that it probably serves to sum up that editor's perception of a fundamental part of Isaiah's preaching.

Another disputed subject concerns the precise nature of the offence. At first sight it looks as though some people — presumably senior officials in the royal administration — were inventing new laws that would give them some advantage over the poor. Despite the expression translated 'write oppressive statutes', however, this seems inherently improbable, even as exaggerated rhetoric. More probably, therefore, it refers rather to the written forms of the administration of justice: the accounts of their decisions and so on.

Either way, however, the really striking thing is that a concern for social justice is said here, without the need for justification, to be superior to the formal elements in the administration of justice, whether in the framing or in the administration of the law. And as if to underline that this is a matter of principle, it is interesting to find that the familiar pair of orphans and widows are again trotted out. Alongside the 'needy' and the 'poor', these are stereotypical of the disadvantaged, as we have seen, and the author's point is not to speak of specific cases but to make the wider point that a matter of principle is here at stake.

There is obviously no direct reference here to the laws from Sinai; they simply do not get mentioned, even though, of course, they include material that we might have supposed was highly relevant to these concerns. Had they been immediately appropriate to the case, we should assume that the writer would have invoked them in his support. As it stands, however, the passage affirms rather that there is a self-authenticating element of natural justice which no amount of administrative manipulation can deflect. It therefore stands as powerful testimony to the belief that the concerns of social justice are somehow instinctively known. They cannot be learnt from the system, because the system is explicitly corrupt. It is just one of those things that we know, and nothing can deny or override it, no matter how formal or apparently authoritative. It verges on a statement that natural law overrides the written law if the two are seen to be in conflict. I conclude, therefore, with some words from Houston, *Contending for Justice*, 93, which summarize one aspect of his analysis of the prophets but which we may reasonably apply more widely as well:

4. Prophetic Justice

In the prophetic texts judgment is normally made on social oppression not according to specific laws, nor by harking back to an imagined past or appealing to a formal pattern of society, but according to moral norms which are accepted universally in all human societies of which we have knowledge, norms which the authors in these texts clearly expect their audiences to share, and which they therefore did not create.

A new element

While conscious that this has only touched on some of the major elements in the eighth-century prophets, I believe that enough has been said to indicate that while each prophet has his own voice and particular areas of concern they are closely comparable in the specific topic that we are investigating. Before concluding this chapter, however, I should like to add a few words about one new element that enters into the prophetic literature later on and which seems to be distinctively Israelite.

In the prophets who come from around the start of the Babylonian exile or soon after, we find that added to the orphan and widow the figure of the 'resident alien' is also joined as someone who should be treated with special kindness within the realm of social justice: 'Act with justice and righteousness … and do no wrong or violence to the alien, the orphan, and the widow …' (Jer. 22:3; cf. 7:6); 'the alien residing within you suffers extortion; the orphan and the widow are wronged in you' (Ezek. 22:7); 'Render true judgments, show kindness and mercy to one another; do not oppress the widow, the orphan, the alien, or the poor' (Zech. 7:9–10; cf. Mal. 3:5). The word is associated a number of times in both Jeremiah and Ezekiel with the fact that those in exile were regarded as 'aliens' in Babylon, so that from their experience they should know to treat others in the same situation with compassion.

The relatively intensive use of the word at this time as well as its collocation with the orphan and widow is also found prominently in the book of Deuteronomy, e.g. 'you shall not deprive a resident alien or an orphan of justice; you shall not take a widow's garment in pledge' (Deut. 24:17). Most frequently this occurs in contexts where positive acts of generosity or kindness are being encouraged, and this goes along with the reminder that 'you' were once aliens in the land of Egypt.

It is difficult to separate these uses in the later prophets and in Deuteronomy, though whether the earlier recollection of the sojourn in Egypt is transferred to the experience in Babylon or *vice versa* is difficult to be sure. It is true that there are a couple of parallel references also in the earlier Book of the Covenant (Exod. 22:21 — linked with the widow and orphan in the next verse — and 23:9[14]) but it is difficult to disagree with the consensus opinion that these have been added under the influence of Deuteronomy;[15] if that is not the case, all one can say is that they had no appreciable influence on Israelite literature or thought until the later period.[16]

---

14 On these, see Houston, *Contending for Justice*, 107–9.

15 See Christoph Bultmann, *Der Fremde im antiken Juda: Eine Untersuchung zum sozialen Typenbegriff 'ger' und seinem Bedeutungswandel in der alttestamentlichen Gesetzgebung* (Forschungen zur Religion und Literatur des Alten und Neuen Testaments 153; Göttingen: Vandenhoeck & Ruprecht, 1992).

16 Cf. van Houten, *The Alien in Israelite Law*, who maintains that the occurrences in Exodus reflect pre-Deuteronomic law but who also argues that the identity of 'the alien' developed between the various legal corpora. Gerson Galil, 'The Hebrew Inscription from Khirbet Qeiyafa/Netaʿim', *UF* 41 (2009), 193–242, finds it twice (once in combination with the widow and orphan and once in combination with the needy and the slave) in his reading of a tenth century inscription from Khirbet Qeiyafa, a site near the Elah valley some 27 kilometres southwest of Jerusalem. The reading of this extremely difficult inscription is far from certain, however. Were Galil's reading correct, it would, of course, be of enormous interest from a number of points of view, but at this early stage of research it seems wise to suspend judgment until other specialists have had time to consider and confirm it; dissenting opinions have already been expressed by Christopher Rollston, 'The Khirbet Qeiyafa Ostracon: Methodological

So far as I am aware, this new element in the familiar group of those who were stereotypically prone to being socially abused is without any parallel elsewhere in the ancient Near East; it seems to be characteristically Israelite or Judean.[17] It appears to have been added on the basis of historical experience and as such it furnishes a significant example of the case we shall reach at the end of our analysis, namely that what is meant by social justice is something that one simply knows inherently to be the case; albeit that inherent knowledge needs to be refined by what one knows of God himself as the supremely just and compassionate one. It is thus an exceedingly valuable addition to our discussion so far, since it both relates to something distinctively 'biblical' and shows up how the development of the understanding of this crucial topic was the result of reflection upon new experiences, which needed to be assimilated into the nation's thinking.

Musings and Caveats', *Tel Aviv* 38 (2011), 67–82, and Alan R. Millard, 'The Ostracon from the Days of David Found at Khirbet Qeiyafa', *Tyndale Bulletin* 62 (2011), 1–13, who, developing a suggestion of E. Cook, thinks that it was most likely just a list of names.

17 Van Houten, *The Alien in Biblical Law*, 34, and Baker, *Tight Fists or Open Hands?*, 177–78, trawl the relevant texts in an attempt to find such a reference, but succeed in showing that effectively there is none.

5

Messianic Justice

In our study so far we have looked at some general issues relating to social justice and at how that is reflected in some dominant elements in the book of Proverbs and in some of the prophets. In this chapter I want to examine what I have called messianic justice. This relates to hopes that the biblical writers may have held regarding the implementation of social justice in the future either by God or by his appointed human agent, whom for convenience rather than in a fully strict manner I am calling the messiah.

This topic overlaps to some extent with what we saw in relation to some of the prophets, because almost inevitably it is the role of the king that is foremost in this regard. We saw, for instance, that Isa. 32:1 seems to speak proverbially of the ideal of kingship when it affirms that 'a king should reign in the interests of righteousness, and princes rule for the furtherance of justice'. Furthermore, in the historical books 2 Sam. 8:15 ('David administered justice and righteousness to all his people') and 1 Kgs 10:9 ('Because the Lord loved Israel for ever, he has made you king to execute justice and righteousness') show that this ideal was realized in the cases of David and Solomon.[1] We may note too the statement about King Josiah in Jer. 22:15: 'Did not your father eat and drink and do justice and righteousness? Then it was well with him'.[2]

---

1 Cf. Smith, *The Fate of Justice and Righteousness*.
2 The role of the king in this regard is discussed more fully in Weinfeld,

5. Messianic Justice

There is no use pretending that the biblical writers were under any illusion that the majority of the kings of Israel and Judah practised these virtues in reality. Both the historical and the prophetic books are full of references that depict a negative portrayal of the kings and their officials in regard to social justice. There is thus a significant element of utopianism in these positive sayings — a depiction of what could be as a futuristic vision to contrast with the harshness of present experience. Precisely because of this, what was thus affirmed in the historical arena, and yet was so often the subject of disappointment, was readily translated into future aspiration, first when a new king came to the throne and then in a more prolonged manner when there was no longer a native king of Judah but when, in the second temple period, the psalms that had given expression to such hopes historically must have come to be understood as referring rather to some future time of restoration.

Psalm 72

Of the several psalms that might be chosen to illustrate this feature, few if any are more powerful than Psalm 72, and so I plan to survey it in more detail as a basis for what will follow later.

The psalm is a prayer to God on behalf of the king. It starts with a firm and clear expression of the wish that God would grant him the ability to administer justice — and that includes social justice in the sense that we have been defining it here in particular:

> Give the king your justice, O God,
>   and your righteousness to a king's son. (Ps. 72:1)

This translation suggests that our familiar word pair is in use here, and certainly we should not be led far astray if we were to follow that impression. In fact, the Hebrew text uses the plural form of the word here rendered 'justice'. Two of the ancient translations

---

Social Justice, ch. 4 (pp. 45–56).

(Septuagint and Peshitta) render as though it were singular, and so many commentators make a very slight emendation to make the text agree with that; certainly, standing in parallel with 'righteousness', one can see the attractiveness of that suggestion. Yet, for that very reason the force of the argument for emending is weakened, since it is easier to imagine that a translator would align a text with what might be expected from elsewhere than that the Hebrew text would be corrupted from the more to the less usual.[3] If the Hebrew plural is correct, then presumably it refers to individual judicial or legal decisions by the king rather than serving as a catch-all phrase for social justice.

However, even if this is so, little is lost from our point of view, since not only does this line encompass our concerns in a wider sense, but in the very next line we find the singular word used in parallel with 'righteousness', so that the general point is made as the basis for the more particular point in the first line:

> May he judge your people with righteousness,
>   and your poor with justice.   (Ps. 72:2)

We may confidently affirm, therefore, that this Psalm is first and foremost a prayer that the king will exercise social justice on God's behalf and that it will reflect God's own standard of what that is.[4]

---

3   The two different positions are adopted in two of the most recent major commentaries: Marvin E. Tate, *Psalms 51–100* (Word Biblical Commentary 20; Dallas, Texas: Word Books, 1990), 219–26, and Frank-Lothar Hossfeld and Erich Zenger, *Psalms 2: A Commentary on Psalms 51–100* (Minneapolis, MN: Fortress, 2005), 201–20.

4   Among many other studies of this Psalm, we may note here in particular Houston, *Contending for Justice*, 138–49, as well as his earlier article: Walter J. Houston, 'The King's Preferential Option for the Poor: Rhetoric, Ideology and Ethics in Psalm 72', *Biblical Interpretation* 7 (1999), 341–67. Houston is sensitive to the ideological bent of the psalm (it 'embodies the ideal that the Davidic dynasty wished to be seen by its subjects to fulfil') which leads to some elements of contradiction and concealment in the text (though it seems to me that some elements of this, at least, may be ascribed

5. Messianic Justice

There seem to be two main elements in the remainder of the Psalm that fill out further what all this involves. In the first place, there can be no doubt that externally it involves this king in international victory and prestige. The prayer is that he will 'have dominion from sea to sea' with his enemies bowing before him in subjection, tribute pouring in to his treasuries and all foreign kings and nations being subservient to him (vv. 8–11). Perhaps unexpectedly, this is regarded as a mark of blessing by them, for the agricultural prosperity that will result from his just rule is something in which they apparently share; they are blessed in him and they pronounce him happy (vv. 15–17). While this picture of superiority may seem to conflict with modern notions of justice, it fits closely with the pattern of thinking that we have already met elsewhere. As in the first part of the book of Isaiah, society is assumed to be hierarchically arranged. If the system is to work ideally, then it is of vital importance that the Davidic king be of unchallenged superiority. This was not merely for his own gratification, however, but in order that, under God as ultimately supreme, he might be in the position of unchallenged security from which he would be able to administer social justice in an unfettered manner.

This needs then to be balanced, secondly, with the heavy emphasis in the Psalm upon the insistence that it is the poor who will be favoured by his just rule. This was already indicated in the programmatic verse 2, cited above. While the poor are explicitly mentioned in the second half of the line (as well as repeatedly later on), it is interesting to note the use of 'your people' as the lead term here, and the term 'people' recurs in vv. 3 and 4 as well. While this is clearly a general term for the king's subjects, it is qualified in two important ways. First, they are primarily God's people, 'your people', as v. 2 states, and secondly the term

---

rather to the gulf between ideal and historical reality). He agrees, however, that the psalm also has 'permanent ethical value', not least when it came to have a more messianic reading after the end of the monarchical period.

is qualified both in this verse and in v. 4 by being closely related with the poor; here, the parallel term is 'your poor', and in v. 4 we read of 'the poor of the people'.

This use of the word, which seems to make its application rather narrower than might at first appear, is not limited to this Psalm. An interesting parallel occurs at Isa. 3:13, for instance:

> The Lord is taking his stand to plead,
> And is standing to exercise judgment on behalf of his people
> (my translation).[5]

As we saw briefly in the previous chapter, this is part of a passage which seems to be applying the lessons of the Song of the Vineyard at the start of Isaiah 5. For our present purposes, we should note that the use of the term 'people' is again narrowed from the population as a whole. At the very least it excludes 'the elders of his people and their leaders' who are mentioned in the next verse as those with whom God is taking issue. Furthermore, although obviously there is a sense in which the language is being used metaphorically, it uses a court image to depict God acting as plaintiff with no reference to any judge, witnesses, verdict or sentence. It thus stands as a graphic depiction of God acting on behalf of the poor among his people without any apparent reference to a law book on which the oppressors are accused or the poor vindicated. Once again, we seem to be more in the realm of natural justice, where the decision on what is right is deemed to be obvious and where God simply moves without the need for further justification to maintain it.

---

5   This translation includes a slight and widely agreed emendation. The received Hebrew text reads 'peoples' rather than 'his people'. I have set out the reasons for favouring the emendation in *Isaiah 1–5*, 265–66. In any case we may note that in v. 15 just later the text has God speaking unequivocally of 'my people' who are said to be being crushed and, in parallel, who are identified with the poor whose faces are being grinded.

5. Messianic Justice

The parallels with our Psalm are clear and abundant. Identical vocabulary is used for the poor (*'aniyyim*, Ps. 72:2; Isa. 3:15), judging (*din*, Ps. 72:2; Isa. 3:13), crushing (*dikka'*, Ps. 72:4; Isa. 3:15) and so on. But the major difference is that whereas in Isaiah God is depicted as acting unilaterally and on his own account, in the Psalm the prayer is that the same standards and procedures will be enacted by the king on God's behalf.

Returning now to the Psalm in its own right and its emphasis on the recipients of social justice, we have seen how this is set out programmatically in the first two verses. The emphasis continues in what follows, however. In v. 4 it is hoped that the king will 'defend the cause of the poor of the people and give deliverance to the needy', while further down in vv. 12–14 the theme is again predominant, speaking of his deliverance of the needy, the poor and those with no helper, of his having pity on them and even of redeeming their life from oppression.

Conversely, there is a muted, but undeniable, acknowledgment that this will also involve the negative task of crushing the oppressor (v. 4) and of delivering from 'oppression and violence' (v. 14). Since these expressions occur in the sections that are dealing with the internal regulation of the nation, these oppressors should certainly be regarded as Judean citizens rather than foreign tyrants. The Psalm alternates in a quite clear and consistent manner between internal and external affairs, so that the referent in each part is not in doubt.

Overall a clear picture emerges from this Psalm of the hopes for a king who stands very much in the place of God on earth, all victorious in his power and yet devoted to the care, depicted in legal terms, of the poor, weak and needy in society. The consequence of such an ideal rule will be the flourishing of righteousness and peace (v. 7) — desirable qualities which we saw were also the subject of aspiration in Isaiah (e.g. Isa. 9:7) — and interestingly it seems to be assumed that agricultural prosperity will also follow automatically (cf. v. 16); indeed he himself is likened in his good effects to that most vital of all natural elements, rain and showers (v. 6).

This latter element perhaps indicates in particular the extent to which the portrait of the king in this Psalm is deliberately expressed to illustrate his role as God's substitute on earth. If we look, for instance, at those Psalms which celebrate the fact that 'The Lord is king' (i.e. the so-called enthronement psalms, to which are usually ascribed Psalms 47, 93, 96–99), it emerges clearly that a major element in what it was thought to mean by saying that God is king is that he is the creator in the sense in which creation was celebrated sometimes in the temple liturgy. This is not the same depiction of creation with which we are familiar from the opening chapters of Genesis but rather an adaptation of earlier Canaanite myths whereby God is regarded as the one who subdued a pre-existing and very threatening chaos. It emphasizes in some respects the fragility of the physical world and takes comfort from the knowledge that God has established it securely and will not allow it to be overwhelmed by a return of the waters which would otherwise engulf the whole.

Closely associated with this is the view that he is also concerned to (re)establish order in the moral or ethical realm, and for this he is depicted as a judge. Not only are 'righteousness and justice … the foundation of his throne' (Ps. 97:2), thus associating this notion with what we have repeatedly seen to be the ideal case in the human realm, but he is depicted more than once as 'coming to judge the world with righteousness, and the peoples with equity' or the like (Pss. 96:13; 98:9). Perhaps unusually to our initial way of thinking, this is depicted as something that should make us and the rest of the created order rejoice. We tend to think of judgment in negative terms, something to be afraid of, because it will involve our being found guilty and so punished in some way. In these Psalms, however, the picture is much closer to that which we have seen already elsewhere, namely that the act of judging is primarily to be regarded as a putting to rights of those things that have gone wrong, which in the social realm is above all the vindication of the faithful poor against the oppression of the senior classes. The assumption here, of course, is that those who sing the Psalms are among that

5. Messianic Justice

faithful community, whether as Israel/Judah as a minor state that frequently suffers at the hands of stronger external enemies or in a later period as groups and individuals who feel the weight of some internal oppression.

There is, furthermore, an inevitably eschatological element to such hopes; they are futuristic, and might be regarded as the Old Testament equivalent of the Lord's prayer: 'thy kingdom come; thy will be done on earth as it is in heaven'. The passionate longing to see that realized perhaps helps explain part of the reason why such closely related hopes were vested in the human king at the time when Psalm 72 was first composed; theological hope was interpreted in human terms.

But of course the time came when there was no longer any king in Israel or Judah. The Psalms were not abandoned, however, but were found to be of sufficient continuing value to be preserved within the Psalter of later times. The only way that we can make sense of this, it seems to me, is to accept that alongside fond memories of earlier days the Psalms came to be understood as giving expression to what might come again, a restoration of the monarchy in some form, but now in the ideal to which Psalm 72 gave expression rather than its previous function as a role-model, more often frustrated than observed, by a currently ruling king. In the very fact of the preservation of these Psalms, therefore, the people continued to affirm their hopes that God would indeed judge the world in righteousness, and that he would do it through the agency of his newly appointed king.[6] It is a messianic hope in all but name.

---

6   This fact may help resolve the long-running dispute as to whether the verbs in the psalm should be construed as jussives or imperfects. The basic form of the psalm as a prayer for the king suggests that 'originally' they were jussives: may the king do this and that. But once there was no longer any king for whom such a prayer might be offered, they came to be understood as indicative, looking forward to some future figure: he will do this and that. Morphologically, a few of the verbal forms are inescapably jussive, suggesting that this was their original force. Most can be taken either way. Those that are exclusively

A developing hope

What does all this add up to in terms of our main quest in this book? The answer, I believe, has to be that the understanding and exercise of social justice by the king, actual or anticipated, is a close reflection of God's own role. In his case, justice and judgment are closely tied, as we have seen, to the fact that he is creator. He established order in the physical world against the forces of chaos, and he may be expected to maintain it similarly in other realms as well. Social justice is thus closely tied to the design of the created order; it is the way that things were meant to be, and one day God will ensure that this is truly the case. And if the king's role is a close reflection of the divine, as I have tried to demonstrate, then it follows that he should know what is just from the same source and in the same manner. In this realm of thought, justice is less an adherence to some written law or the like but rather is the discernment of the principles that underlie creation. In fact, I should argue, it comes as close as we can imagine to the principles that we saw, albeit at a different social level, in Proverbs and elsewhere.

This conclusion receives support, I believe, from some of the more traditional, classic messianic passages in the prophets. I have already touched on the opening verses of Isaiah 9 in connection with the prophetic vision and so need only observe here that, as with Psalm 72, so in this case the likelihood is that material which in its origin gave expression to the hopes vested in the birth of a new royal child came in later times to be projected forward to a child yet to be born.

As I have sought to show in more detail elsewhere, however, this is only one passage in Isaiah among a number which seem to be related in this regard, even though they

---

imperfect in their present form are only so by the inclusion of certain vowel letters, which would not have been used when the psalm was first written. We may assume without difficulty that, as with all vowel letters, they were added scribally at a later date, in this instance, therefore, at a time when the psalm was already being read predictively.

5. Messianic Justice

may have been written at very different times and in widely varying circumstances.[7] The messianic passage in Isa. 11:1–5 is by no means unrelated ('with righteousness he shall judge the poor, and decide with equity for the meek of the earth'), and the proverbial Isa. 32:1 has also been seen to align closely with these ideals.

My interest here, however, concerns rather the development of this theme in exilic and post-exilic times, as reflected in the second half of the book.

That justice is the dominant theme in the first of the so-called servant songs is evident from the fact that its implementation is anticipated no less than three times in four verses:

> Here is my servant, whom I uphold,
>   my chosen, in whom my soul delights;
> I have put my spirit upon him;
>   he will bring forth justice to the nations.
> He will not cry or lift up his voice,
>   or make it heard in the street;
> a bruised reed he will not break,
>   and a dimly burning wick he will not quench;
>   he will faithfully bring forth justice.
> He will not grow faint or be crushed
>   until he has established justice in the earth;
> and the coastlands wait for his teaching.   (Isa. 42:1–4)

In discussions of this passage, commentators in the past have offered an astonishingly wide variety of understandings of what is meant by justice here. I have found, for instance, such renderings as 'religion', 'truth', 'the principles of true religion' and 'revealed law', as well as the suggestion that it refers more narrowly in its present context to the judgment or verdict of the law court in the various 'trial scenes' that are imaginatively depicted in the surrounding passages.

---

7   See Williamson, *Variations on a Theme*.

In my opinion, none of this is justified. The servant in this passage is undoubtedly depicted in royal terms. While most of the significant elements in the depiction of his person and role here can be paralleled elsewhere by more than one office holder (priest, prophets, and so on), the only one of whom they are all valid is the king.

In addition, quite a few of these features are applied to Israel in the previous chapter (see especially Isa. 41:8–10). It therefore looks as though the otherwise unnamed servant in chapter 42 is being closely identified with Israel in her ideal condition, and that this ideal Israel is depicted as royal — as in some sense a king. (This fits also with what is stated later in Isa. 55:3.) We may therefore assume that this passage is telling us in a creative and fresh manner of Israel's new role on the international scene.

Now, as soon as we recognize that the underlying figure is depicted as a king, it becomes obvious and natural that 'justice' should mean what it has meant previously in all the other passages we have examined. In Israel the king constituted, so to speak, the ultimate court of appeal, and he was responsible for the impartial administration of justice. In this new setting, however, that is taken up and reapplied in new circumstances. We are now in a world where there is only one universal God, and part of Israel's new task as servant is to mediate his light and salvation to the ends of the earth, as the continuation of our passage in 42:6, to go no further, makes clear. Among the nations, furthermore, there is a crying need for justice of the sort that we have seen the king was encouraged to implement previously within Israel, but now accommodated to these new circumstances. Quite what that means in detail is left unsaid, but it is clear that on the one hand it is something that the nations anticipate with positive emotions (that is the force of the words 'wait for' in the last line of the passage) and on the other that, without noise or fanfare, it benefits those who are metaphorically depicted as bruised reeds and dimly burning wicks.

5. Messianic Justice

What seems to me to be of paramount importance for our topic is that we see here that such justice, within which I include social justice, will not look the same in every circumstance, but will adapt certain fundamental principles to the very new circumstances which are opened up by the developments in Israel's history. This helps us to understand that the kind of language we have been studying throughout this book is not an inflexible rule to be applied woodenly and unchangingly in every circumstance. The problem with that approach to interpretation is that before long we find that the circumstances have changed so much that in fact we cannot apply them at all, so that we come to the point of just leaving them aside neglected. But if the Old Testament itself demonstrates that it is advancing underlying principles that are illustrated by application in a variety of different circumstances, then we realize that we cannot escape the responsibility of thinking how they might be applied in turn in our own very different world.[8]

As a further example of the same point I might refer to the final great messianic passage in Isaiah, namely 61:1–3:

> The spirit of the Lord God is upon me,
>   because the Lord has anointed me;
> he has sent me to bring good news to the oppressed,
>   to bind up the broken-hearted,
> to proclaim liberty to the captives,
>   and release to the prisoners;
> to proclaim the year of the Lord's favour,
>   and the day of vengeance of our God;
>   to comfort all who mourn;

---

8 This is not unlike the approach to biblical ethics that has been advocated under the banner of 'paradigm' by Wright in a number of his publications; see, for instance, Christopher J.H. Wright, *Living as the People of God: The Relevance of Old Testament Ethics* (Leicester: Inter-Varsity Press, 1983), and *God's People in God's Land: Family, Land and Property in the Old Testament* (Carlisle: Paternoster, 1990, reprinted 1997).

> to provide for those who mourn in Zion—
>> to give them a garland instead of ashes,
>> the oil of gladness instead of mourning,
>>> the mantle of praise instead of a faint spirit.

This remarkable passage, coming towards the end of the book of Isaiah as a whole, seems to me to gather up the vocabulary which relates to most of the agents of salvation in the previous chapters. For instance, for endowment with the spirit, see 42:1; for being anointed, see 45:1; for bringing good news, see 40:9, 41:27, 52:7; and so on. I have set this out in full elsewhere as the basis for a case that, far from presenting this character as one or another of the book's characters, it in fact picks up, reaffirms and maintains the continuing validity of all the previous promises, many of which seemed to have run into the sand in the disappointing days that followed the first return to Jerusalem after the exile.[9] It is thus genuinely messianic, not only because it is one of the very few passages explicitly to refer to the character's being anointed (in this case, I believe, as a way of resuming the role of the anointed Cyrus in 45:1), but also because it re-presents in a synthetic manner all the different elements that had been promised in separate and different circumstances in what preceded.

What I should like to draw attention to here in addition, however, is the equally striking observation that those to whom this character will minister seem also to be an amalgamation of all the differing situations of distress that the book envisages: oppressed, broken-hearted, captives, prisoners, all who mourn and those of faint spirit. Self-evidently these are not descriptions of a single individual or group in just one position of need. The concerns vary from political to social to emotional to economic and to other situations. Both the agent of deliverance and the one delivered, therefore, are compiled and compounded amalgamations.

---

9   *Variations on a Theme*, 174–88.

5. Messianic Justice

No wonder Jesus is depicted in Luke 4:16–21 as claiming the fulfilment of this passage in the ministry that he was about to inaugurate. But even his fulfilment does not mean that the scripture's challenge and impact was thereby exhausted; it remained and remains open. One cannot earth this passage in a single historical situation or even two, but must regard it rather as an idealized expression of what the exercise of social justice could embrace in the insignificant Persian province of Judah, in Roman-occupied Palestine of centuries later, or ... There is an unlegislated flexibility here that should enable you to fill in the dots for yourself.

6

He Has Shown You What is Good

How, then, should we summarize the gist of what we have tried to explore in this book?

Allow me first to stress something on which I have hardly touched at all, and that is that of course there are many elements of the pentateuchal law which also have a practical concern for social justice. David Baker has recently published a large and significant analysis of this subject which makes clear that, as elsewhere in the ancient Near East, there was a legislative concern in this realm as much as in many others.[1]

While that remains valuable as a statement of intent, however, it leaves us with some quandaries which I have tried to tackle in a somewhat fresh manner. First, the very fact that the law codes had to be revised on several occasions, as I indicated in chapter 2, means that it must have been difficult to know quite how to apply them as the nature and circumstances of the Israelite state changed over the centuries. Some aspects of social justice were closely tied, as we have seen, to the proper exercise of the law, but this itself was the subject of enormous variation, so that the laws can only be illustrative of certain particularities, and these are often difficult to unravel because of the many uncertainties about history and dating.

---

[1] Baker, *Tight Fists or Open Hands?*

6. He Has Shown You What is Good

Second, we have seen time and again that the wisdom writers, the prophets and the psalmists all had a passionate concern for social justice but remarkably they did not appeal to the law to describe it, to explain how it had been flouted or even to undergird it as a concern that was shared by God. Henry Gehman wrote on this subject many years ago (when it was decidedly out of fashion). He started his analysis with a reference to Mic. 3:1, which includes the phrase 'to know justice', and he commented that this refers to 'something more than a thorough knowledge of the rules of justice and the verdicts of justice; it refers, in fact, to that love for what is right, a concern with the being right of the law'.[2]

Third, there are many elements that we might consider to fall within the purview of social justice to which these writers also make reference but which are completely absent from the law. It is obvious, therefore, that any approach to the question of how we know what social justice is which thinks that we can reach an answer solely by our knowledge of the law will end up by being woefully inadequate.

The upshot must be, therefore, that to stress the centrality of revealed law in connection with social justice as discussed in the bulk of the Old Testament writings is to bark up the wrong tree. We need to start again.

In place of the law, therefore, I have tried to show that other closely inter-related sources of inspiration for understanding this topic are more prominent.

In a sense the underlying principle that the various writers have displayed is that in this matter people should try to imitate God according the way that they best know him. Naturally, this is a conclusion which stems from a standpoint of faith, as we should say today, but that was hardly an issue, so far as we can tell, for our writers in their day. In what capacity they thought they knew God best will have varied. We have seen, for instance,

---

2 Gehman, 'Natural Law and the Old Testament'.

that Isaiah pressed upon his fellow Jerusalemite leading citizens the consequences of understanding God as king. For others, as represented in the book of Proverbs, God was the one who had created the world in wisdom, while for some of the psalmists he was the creator as the one who initiated and maintained cosmic stability and order. Naturally, these are all images to some degree, and that they strive to give expression to some higher reality may be asserted on the basis of the number of times we have seen how expressions in one realm seem to be closely echoed in another.

Further down, the consequences of this rather abstract conclusion may be seen from the way in which the writers' epistemology—how they know what they know—derives from these fundamental convictions. The way God has created the world is to be discerned by observation and experience—and that, I need hardly add, is something which may be refined over the course of time. Similarly, not only in Israel but also more widely in the ancient world there was a clear sense that part of the duties of rule was the care of the disadvantaged. This was not to be put into effect through interference in the regular business of loans and dealing but rather by way of attention to those more particular cases where either the system was being subverted in some way—oppression—or the people involved had lost their natural human representatives (hence the orphans and widows) so that others needed to act beneficially on their behalf.

But how should people know just how to act in particular circumstances? On what resources could they draw for guidance? Here, my contention throughout has been to try to show that these writers work from an assumption that ultimately anyone thinking rightly about social justice should know instinctively what is right. If it is self-evidently wrong to get drunk and self evidently stupid to try to plough the sea with oxen, then it is deemed equally natural to show compassion on those who are less advantaged than we ourselves.

That simple conclusion needs to be qualified, of course. First, our sense of what is obviously right is itself subject to change

6. He Has Shown You What is Good

as historical circumstances change. The introduction of the resident alien to the pairing of orphan and widow is just one, albeit a very striking, example of this factor.

Second, there seems to be presupposed a need for rigorous honesty in all such calculations. The Old Testament is well aware, and illustrates on many occasions, that people can deceive themselves into thinking that their practices are justified when to all outward appearances they are clearly deeply mistaken. Walter Brueggemann has some chilling words of warning on just this point: 'unless it is seen as pronouncedly Yahwistic … [creation faith] is open for ideological abuse. This may be true politically when the order of creation is equated with a preferred social order, such as by appeal to "natural law." We have ample evidence of the destructiveness of such an equation'.[3]

And third, Israel's understanding of God deepened and became more refined through time, resulting both from historical experience and from commentary on it by those with especially heightened sensitivity.[4]

But with all those caveats, the advantages of this way of looking at our topic seem to be considerable, even if frighteningly challenging. For we do not stand outside this continuum of the experience of the people of God, but as Christians we are more privileged even than the people of Israel were in our knowledge of God's compassion and our inheritance of their interpretative writings. Young children seem to have an untaught habit of

---

3 Walter Brueggemann, *Theology of the Old Testament: Testimony, Dispute, Advocacy* (Minneapolis: Fortress, 1997), 163.

4 It is relevant to note in this connection, however, that God is himself depicted in a number of passages as one who performs and is concerned with justice and righteousness; cf. Weinfeld, *Social Justice*, 179–214; Houston, *Contending for Justice*, 203–25. My somewhat humanistic-sounding remarks above may thus themselves be seen theologically as *imitatio dei*. Jackson's comments, '"Law" and "Justice" in the Bible', 223, are apposite: 'What is the supposed source of the "justice" these judges are to apply? … a mixture of custom and personal intuition, the latter being presented as inspired by God'.

declaring that what their parents do from time to time 'just isn't fair'. They may be wrong in their appraisal of the situation because they do not have enough knowledge to assess the situation correctly. But their instinct, it seems to me, remains sound.

Their parents in turn may well have behaved in ways that are more to their own advantage than their children's in given circumstances, but that is not always the case; there remain situations where what seems unfair to the child is in fact both loving and ultimately more fair. At the simplest level, the child will grow up and learn to see things differently.

Amartya Sen opens the Preface to his major book on justice with a reminder of a saying of Pip in Charles Dickens's *Great Expectations*: 'In the little world in which children have their existence, there is nothing so finely perceived and finely felt, as injustice.' Sen continues 'But the strong perception of manifest injustice applies to adult human beings as well. What moves us, reasonably enough, is not the realization that the world falls short of being completely just—which few of us expect—but that there are clearly remediable injustices around us which we want to eliminate'.[5]

Is it so inconceivable that as children of a heavenly father we as individuals and as communities might not also be growing up, taking on board the hard lessons of history from the days of Israel on, learning from the multifarious experiences of those who have preceded us and passed on wisdom as they saw it then, but ultimately, with honesty, learning that some sound principles are better applied in one way than another? To that process of education, prophets, wisdom writers, psalmists and others play an indispensible role.

But our world is not the same as theirs, so that to be true to their insights we have constantly to rethink and refashion the true sense of social justice. What that might involve will in like manner be informed by the New as well as by the Old Testament,

---

5   Sen, *The Idea of Justice*, vii.

6. He Has Shown You What is Good

and also by the many positive and negative lessons shown by honest Christians through some two thousand years of attempts at faithful living. As we look back, we realize that people did not get it right all of the time. Socially acceptable standards of a previous era may be abhorrent to us today; slavery is a standard example. Our sense of Christian 'fairness' is inevitably, therefore, under constant revision, and future generations may well look back in equal horror at some of the accepted standards of our own times.

This realization should not put us off, however. If we adopt a legalistic approach to social justice, we may conclude that we have not 'broken the law'; there will not be the breaking of any one biblical command that can be laid to our charge. But such an approach would exalt a passive life of self-satisfied pietism above the biblical trumpet call for justice and righteousness in imitation of the divine king, an abdication of Christian responsibility to love in a transformative manner, a denial of the basic biblical principles on which our faith is supposedly grounded. We shall almost certainly make mistakes as we seek to practise a proactive life of implementing social justice where we are and as best we can according to the vision that God has given in scripture and the church. But that must not be allowed to become a barrier. If we fail to do so, we may end up ourselves by running horses on the rocks and ploughing the sea with oxen.

> *He has told you, O mortal, what is good;*
> *and what does the Lord require of you*
> *but to do justice, and to love kindness,*
> *and to walk humbly with your God?* (Micah 6:8)

Bibliography

This is not a full bibliography of the subject nor of the various works cited in the footnotes of the present book. Rather, it is an introductory list of books of particular relevance to the subject of the book as a whole.

David L. Baker, *Tight Fists or Open Hands? Wealth and Poverty in Old Testament Law* (Grand Rapids, Michigan: Eerdmans, 2009)
John Barton, *Ethics and the Old Testament* (London: SCM, 1998)
John Barton, *Understanding Old Testament Ethics: Approaches and Explorations* (Louisville, KY: Westminster John Knox, 2003)
Carol J. Dempsey, *Justice: A Biblical Perspective* (St. Louis, Missouri: Chalice Press, 2008)
Léon Epsztein, *Social Justice in the Ancient Near East and the People of the Bible* (London: SCM, 1986)
Richard A. Horsley, *Covenant Economics: A Biblical Vision of Justice for All* (Louisville, KY: Westminster John Knox, 2009)
Walter J. Houston, *Contending for Justice: Ideologies and Theologies of Social Justice in the Old Testament* (Library of Hebrew Bible/Old Testament Studies 428; London: T & T Clark, 2006)
Walter J. Houston, *Justice – The Biblical Challenge* (London: Equinox, 2010)
Christiana van Houten, *The Alien in Israelite Law* (Journal for the Study of the Old Testament, Supplement Series 107; Sheffield: Sheffield Academic Press, 1991)
Bruce V. Malchow, *Social Justice in the Hebrew Bible: What Is New and What Is Old?* (Collegeville, Minnesota: Liturgical Press, 1996)
Enrique Nardoni, *Rise Up, O Judge: A Study of Justice in the Biblical World* (Peabody, Massachusetts: Hendrickson Publishers, 2004)
J. David Pleins, *The Social Visions of the Hebrew Bible: A Theological Introduction* (Louisville, KY: Westminster John Knox, 2001)
Moshe Weinfeld, *Social Justice in Ancient Israel and in the Ancient Near East* (Jerusalem: Magnes, 1995)
Christopher J.H. Wright, *Living as the People of God: The Relevance of Old Testament Ethics* (Leicester: Inter-Varsity Press, 1983)

Index of Biblical References

Genesis
18:19	19
18:20–21, 25	20
19:13	20

Exodus
3:7	20
20–23	37
21:2–11	39
22:21	88
23:9	88
24:7	37

Leviticus
25:39–42	39

Deuteronomy
10:18	16
15:12–17	39
24:17	88
32:14	78

1 Samuel
9:16	20

2 Samuel
8:15	66, 90

1 Kings
10:9	90

2 Kings
22–23	38

Nehemiah
5	79
5:1	20

Job
29:12–16	14–15

Psalms
9:8	18
22:12	78
33:5	17
45:6–7	18
47	96
58:1	18
72:1	91
72:2	92–93, 95
72:3	93
72:4	93–95
72:6, 7	95
72:8–11	93
72:12–14	95
72:15–17	93
72:16	95
82:1–4	16
89:14	17
93	96
94:4–6	16

Psalms cont'd

96–99	96
96:13	96
97:2	96
98:9	18, 96
99:4	18

Proverbs

1–9	45–47
1:1	45
1:3	18, 49
1:8	50
2:1	50
2:9	18, 51
3:1	50
3:9–10	62
3:11–12	57
4:1, 10, 20	50
5:1	50
6:6–11	58
6:20	50
7:1	50
8	60
8:15–16	54, 69
8:20	53
10:1	45, 56
10:2–3	53
10:2, 3	58
10:4, 5	57
10:19	59
11:1, 4, 19	53
11:24–25	61
12:5	51, 53
12:17	53
13:21	53
13:23	53, 61
13:24	57
13:25	53
14:21	61
14:31	62
15:6	53
15:25	62

Proverbs cont'd

16:8	51
16:10	69
16:11	53
16:13	69
16:23	53
17:5	62
17:15, 26	53
18:5	52
18:28	53
19:17	62
20:8	69
20:10, 23	53
20:26	69
21:3	51
21:13	20
21:15	51
22:2	62
22:9	61
22:22–23	62
22:28	31
23:10	31
23:13–14	57
24:23	45, 53
24:24	53
25:1	45
25:5	54
28:27	61
29:4	69
29:7	49, 53
29:13	62
29:14	69
31:4–5	69, 84
31:9	52

Isaiah

1:15	67
1:16–17	16
1:17	66
1:21–26	83
1:21–23	68
1:21	49, 66, 67

Index of Biblical References

Isaiah cont'd

1:23	69, 72
2:13	78
3:13–15	68
3:13	94–95
3:15	72, 95
5:1–7	68
5:7	20, 66, 68
5:8–24	83
5:22–23	83
5:25	85
6	70
6:1	71
9:7	69, 95
9:12, 17, 21	85
10:1–4	84–85
11:1–5	99
11:4	18
16:5	17
28:7	84
28:16–17	67
32:1	69, 90, 99
33:15	18
40:9	102
41:8–10	100
41:27	102
42:1–4	99
42:1	102
42:6	100
45:1	102
45:19	18
52:7	102
55:3	100
61:1–3	101–2

Jeremiah

7:5–6	15
7:6	87
9:24	17
16:5	81

Jeremiah cont'd

22:3	15, 87
22:15	90

Ezekiel

18:5–9	16–17
22:7	87
27:6	78
39:18	78

Hosea

2:19	75–76

Amos

1–2	81
1:3, 6, 9, 13	36
2:8	84
4:1–3	77
4:1	84
5:6, 7, 10–12, 14–15	73
5:21–24	74
6:1–7	80–82
6:6	84
6:7	81–82
6:12	73–75

Micah

3:1	105
6:8	109
7:9	76
7:14	78

Zechariah

7:9–10	15, 87
11:2	78

Malachi

3:5	87

Luke

4:16–21	103

General Index

Abraham, 19–21
alien, resident, 87–89
Amarna letters, 29
Amenemhet, 30
Amenemope, Instruction of, 30
Aqhat ('Aqhatu), 26

Babylon, 87–88
Baker, David, 104
Barr, James, 33
Barton, John, 34–35
Bashan, 78
Book of the Covenant, 37, 88
Brueggemann, Walter, 107

Canaan, 25
Crouch, Carly, 40
Cyrus, 102

Danilu, King, 26
David, 66
Dickens, Charles, 108
Drinking, 83–84

Egypt, 9–31
enthronement psalms, 96

fairtrade, 80

Gehman, Henry, 23, 105
Golan Heights, 78
Gudea, Cylinders of, 28

Hammurabi, law-code of, 27–28

Houston, Walter, 46, 78, 86

Job, 58
judge, 96
justice and righteousness, 13–18

Keret (Kirta), King, 26
Khirbet Qeiyafa, 88
kindness, 17–18

land tenure, 40
Lord's prayer, 97

Ma'at, 54–55
McConville, Gordon, 19
Malchow, Bruce, 46
marzeach, 81–82
Mein, Andrew, 17
Merikare, Instruction of, 30
Messiah, 90
Miranda, José, 14

natural justice, 23, 32–36, 75
natural law, 56

orphan and widow, 24–32

patronage, 79
Phoenicia, 32
Pip, 108
Pleins, David, 46
poor, 61
priestly law, 37

Queen of Sheba, 66

Index

Sen, Amartya, 108
servant, 99–100
slave laws, 38
Sodom and Gomorrah, 20–21
Solomon, 66

Ugarit, 25–27, 29, 31
Ur-namma, 28

Uru-inimgina of Lagash, 28

Weinfeld, Moshe, 13
Whybray, Norman, 46–47
Wisdom, 56
women of Samaria, 77–79

Zion, 67–68, 72

www.ingramcontent.com/pod-product-compliance
Lightning Source LLC
Chambersburg PA
CBHW070632220426
R18178600001B/R181786PG43193CBX00017B/23